Renovate a Sailboat
and
Cross the Atlantic

by George DuBose

and thanks to those
who helped along the way:
Don Vanderveer
Charles Schwendler
Andy Heermans
Rudy Ratsep
Bennett Jucofsky
Rick Doherty
Ben Morris
Dominic Dreyfus
Bill Craig
Jim Ledogar
Robert Jones
Leah Crandall
Barry Nitzberg
Omar Hernandez
Bob DuBose
Dr. med. Susanne DuBose

All text ©2014 by George DuBose
Photos courtesy Skylark's crew

All rights reserved. No part of this book may be reproduced or transmitted in any form or by any means electronic or mechanical, including photocopying, recording, or any information storage and retrieval system, without permission in writing from the author.

"Renovate a Sailboat and
Cross the Atlantic"
First Edition
ISBN: 978-0-9889-2348-5

Printed in the United States of America.
Library of Congress cataloging-in-publication data

for more information contact:
boss@george-dubose.com
please visit: www.george-dubose.com

Other books by George DuBose
"I Speak Music - Ramones" (English Edition)
ISBN 978-0-9889-2340-9
"Hablo Musica - Ramones" (Edición En Español)
ISBN 978-0-9889-2341-6
"I Speak Music - Hip Hop - Old School Volume One"
]ISBN 978-0-9889-2342-3
"I Speak Music - Hip Hop - Old School Volume Two"
ISBN 978-0-9889-2343-0
"I Speak Music - Hip Hop - Volume Three"
ISBN 978-0-9889-2344-3
"Eu Falo Música – Ramones" - (Primeira Edição)
ISBN 978-0-9889-2345-4
"The Big Book of Hip-Hop Photography" (First Edition)
ISBN 978-0-9889-2346-1
Parlo Musica - Ramones (prima edizione)
ISBN 978-0-9889-2347-8

Foreword

As I was finishing this book, I happened to visit Amazon.com and searched the name of one of my favorite contemporary marine writers, Capt. Fatty Goodlander. Capt. Goodlander writes a monthly column for *Cruising World,* a US publication that used to be one of my favorite sailing magazines, until they started focussing on multi-million dollar catamarans and charter "dashes" through paradise.

Capt. Goodlander writes with a lot of humor and from the point of view of a sea gypsy. To my horror, I saw that the Captain had written a book about buying a boat on the cheap, renovating her and then sailing around the world. Practically the same topics of my long-planned book about buying, renovating and sailing *Skylark* across the Atlantic.

I had to buy Capt. Fatty's book *"Buy, Outfit and Sail"*. Not only do I enjoy his style of writing and point of view, but wanted to see what he had actually had in mind.

I searched his book on Amazon.de, since I am living in Germany. Nada.

I searched Amazon.co.uk and "Voila!", when I received his book purchased through Amazon.co.uk, I was surprised to see that it was printed in Germany by Amazon Distribution.

I have also been publishing on demand and have been using Amazon's printing services of

Create Space to publish my books of music photography and the stories behind the photos.

To my relief, Capt. Goodlander's book isn't the same as this one, although the topics are similar, Capt. Fatty and I have different points of view and approach the same subject differently. The Good Captain illuminates how to find a damaged or derelict boat and how to negotiate the purchase. He tells how to "put out the word" that one is trying to get a bluewater boat put together without spending a dime, or not more than a "pocket full of pennies".

He gives explicit instructions about how to get discounts from chandleries, ways to use non-marine materials to replace expensive items for a few cents on the dollar. How to avoid overpaying for anything and obtain donations from other sailors who have too much redundant or unnecessary gear. Captain Fatty's book is very well written and a great read. He has been a professional sea gypsy and writer all his life and his career as a freelance writer has perhaps, forced him to be more creative and innovative in his renovations.

When I decided to buy a "new" boat and replace my Pearson 26, I knew I wanted a Pearson 36. There weren't many on the market, in fact there were only two. I had to spend more than a "pocket full of pennies" to get the boat of my dreams, but I had access to enough money to buy the boat and planned to spend an equal amount on the renovation. Rather than scrounge, beg and borrow a long list of equipment, time constraints, the great leaps in technology development led me to consider my purchases on the basis of quality and safety.

I was rebuilding *Skylark,* 35 years old at the time, to modern standards, preferring to replace equipment and appliances whose age and maintenance history was unknown. I was not only planning on crossing the Atlantic at least once to get her to Europe, I was planning on doing extensive cruising around Europe with my family and wanted *Skylark* to be able to "handle anything" that Mother Nature would throw at her. She certainly isn't over-equipped, but she does have systems that require diligence and observation.

When my extensive research led me to consider a piece of safety equipment, ie. liferaft, storm sails, sea anchors and drogues, jacklines and harnesses, price was never considered. Of course, when I had decided on a particular piece of equipment, however pricey, I would shop the world over for the cheapest price or deepest discount.

Since you have already bought this book, I can't recommend any book as highly as Capt. Fatty Goodlander's "Buy, Outfit and Sail". That doesn't preclude, "Upgrading the Cruising Sailboat" by Dan Spurr, "This Old Boat" by Dan Casey or any books by Dan Casey or Nigel Calder.

Unless you are having your refit done at Derecktor's Shipyard and have access to the highly trained and experienced staff there, do what I did and read, read, read and then read some more.

Besides reading all of these books cover to cover more than once, I had access to several "mentors" at the boatyard in East Hampton, NY. Don Vanderveer, the owner of Three Mile Marina on Three Mile Harbor had been working on boats since he worked on ships at the Brooklyn Navy Yard during WWII, Charles Schwendler, a Mercedes, boat and certified airplane mechanic, Bennett Jucofsky, a marine equipment salesman and Sam Story, the owner of Three Mile Harbor Marina.

The extensive electrical renovations were led by Andrew Heermans, an audio engineer who also had a good knowledge of electronics, their circuits and he has extremely professional working practices. The unnamed, self-designated first Mate, Jerry Hodgens, the ocean tug captain, my college pal Rick Doherty, Omar Hernandez, who dove under *Skylark* when a milk crate full of new stainless steel deck fittings slid off the deck into the water, all deserve a big thank you. Bill Craig and Bob DuBose, who fed me and my crew after our 12-14 hour work marathons and many of my friends at the boatyard, who were of infinite help. I want to thank all of these guys for helping me make a safe boat even safer.

Acquisition and Renovation

The Purchase

I moved to Europe in 1998, leaving my 1970 Pearson 26 in a boatyard on Long Island. After a few years of shuttling back and forth in the summer to visit the boat, I decided it was time to upgrade to a larger vessel in order to make room for my German wife and two young boys. We needed a boat in Europe that could accommodate all four of us, allow us to cook on board and I thought the possibility of having a hot shower on board would a big wife pleaser.

Being a big fan of Pearsons and well aware of their potential for speed and famous robust construction, I began searching for a Pearson 36-1. There are a number of yacht manufacturers that built yachts capable of crossing oceans and the price for a 70s-era boat was well within my budget. Pearson, Bristol, Catalina, are just a few of the builders that have been around for quite a while and a search for a fixer-upper will find something for every budget and level of refitting skills.

I found *Skylark*, a Pearson 36-1 on eBay in 2007, there was only one other sister-ship on the market at that time and my decision was between a 1972 and a 1973 model. The '72 was listed for $25,000 and had an original Atomic Four gasoline engine and the 1973 was listed at $40,000 and had a new Yanmar diesel. The cost of installing a diesel made the boats about equal in price and I had doubts about my skill level of engine installation. I had refit my Pearson 26 in 1990 and am fairly handy with fiberglass work, caulking and wood work, so finding a slightly abused boat wouldn't put me off.

Skylark was lying in Connecticut and through Boat/US, I contacted a surveyor located near the 1973 Pearson. Before he sent me the results of the survey, he emailed me and asked me to call him before he wrote up his survey. He told me that the boat had a lot of problems. When pressed for details, he told me that none of the "advertised" electronics were connected and he wasn't able to test any of them. He went on to say that the chainplates had been leaking for sometime and there was water damage to the interior.

When I got the survey and carefully read the details, I realized that 1.) all the electronics were quite dated and the new technology with radar and other electronics had made a quantum leap since the 70s, 2.) leaking chainplates could be re-caulked, 3.) the standing rigging was going to be replaced anyway. So without even seeing *Skylark* myself, I bought the boat. Didn't even dicker on the price. I will never forget the previous owner telling me to hold off on the pickup, because he wanted to put the carpeting back in the cabin. I told him not to bother.

A couple of buddies picked up the boat in Connecticut and sailed her over to the Three Mile Boatyard in Long Island's Three Mile Harbor, north of East Hampton, NY.

When I arrived in July 2007, a month after buying the boat and before I even entered the cabin, I saw that the old non-selftailing Lewmar winches were going to be the first things to be replaced. I put no limit on the budget for new electronics, sails or to replace dated equipment. I guesstimated that I would be spending at least what I paid for the boat, but I knew that a tweaked P-36 would be an awesome boat and worth whatever money I spent on the renovation.

The first thing I did was contact Defender Marine and West Marine, two of the biggest online chandleries in the US. I knew from some of the professional shipwrights that if you contacted these companies and told them that you were going to be spending in excess of $10,000 with them, they would give trade discounts on top of their already discounted prices.

I also knew that the euro vs. the US dollar exchange rate, plus the fact that marine supplies are severely overpriced in Europe, meant that my best bet was going to be; buy everything for the refit and do all the work in the US. Purchases from these US online chandleries also meant that on top of the deep discounts, there would be no sales tax. In Europe, the sales tax is between 19% and 25% on top of the manufacturer's suggested retail prices. I figured I would be saving half of what this work would cost me in Europe.

The to-do list was longer than both my arms. An obvious priority was to replace the original Perko circuit panel that used fuses. I contacted Andy Heermans, who was a recording engineer,

The only thing new about Skylark was her Awlgrip® paint job. The locks in The Netherlands and Scotland's Caledonian Canal soon took care of that.

Actually, the Yanmar 3GM30F had only 100 hours and was five years old. The PO didn't travel.

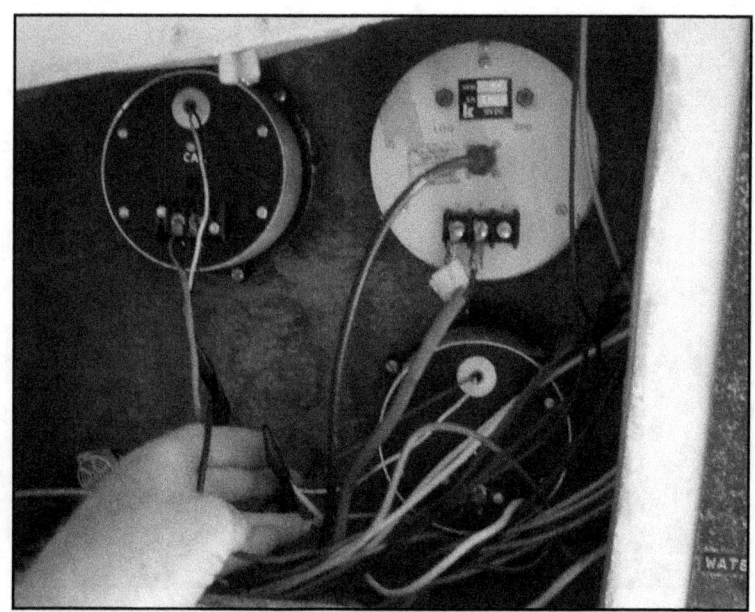

All the wiring was old and technically outdated. We pulled every wire and cable out of the boat and replaced it all with high quality material from Pacer Marine.

but I knew was also a crack electrician. When he surveyed the electrical system, he pointed out that all the original wiring was 35 years old and the copper strands were quite large and untinned.

He found Pacer Marine, a new company that offered a product line that was equal to or better - but less expensive - than the popular, but over-priced Ancor electric products. We decided to replace all the wiring on the entire boat with a larger gauge, finer and tinned strands.

The connectors that Pacer offers have built-in heat shrink tubing and when connected actually snap together producing a waterproof connection.

The original alcohol oven had been replaced

The original circuit panel used glass fuses and had seen better days. It was replaced with a modular circuit panel by Blue Sea with an amp meter to measure current draw.

The new Blue Sea circuit panel developed a loose contact in one of the circuit breakers and Blue Sea FedEx'd me a new one overnight to Germany! That's service!

with a small household icebox that was totally unsuitable for use in a seaway. If you opened the door on a starboard tack, the icebox would have emptied itself all over the cabin sole. An Eno Gasgone three burner stove and oven was installed in its place.

The original water heater was not even tested, it was replaced with an Isomat 6 gallon unit that was plumbed to the engine for heating the water with the hot water from the engine and as the unit was available in 120 or 220 volts, all that would be necessary to convert to 220v would be to change a $40 heating coil. A holding tank was installed with a "Y" connection.

The house batteries were a story of their own. When I first saw the two auto batteries on their "shelf", I wondered how difficult it was going to be to get rid of that shelf. After lifting the batteries out, noticing that there were no tie downs or straps securing them, the shelf just lifted as well. I was shocked. The thin Masonite particle board that separate the lazarette storage from the fuel tank, steering cables and engine was gone, one good heel to port and the batteries would have tumbled onto the engine or the stuffing box.

I bought some 3/4" 11-ply plywood and epoxied pieces for a new battery shelf together, effectively doubling the thickness of the new shelf to 1-1/2". This shelf was bolted to the bulkhead and glassed to the hull. The shelf would also support the new bolted down water heater. One of my

Open this home style refrigerator on starboard tack and one would see the contents all over the cabin sole.

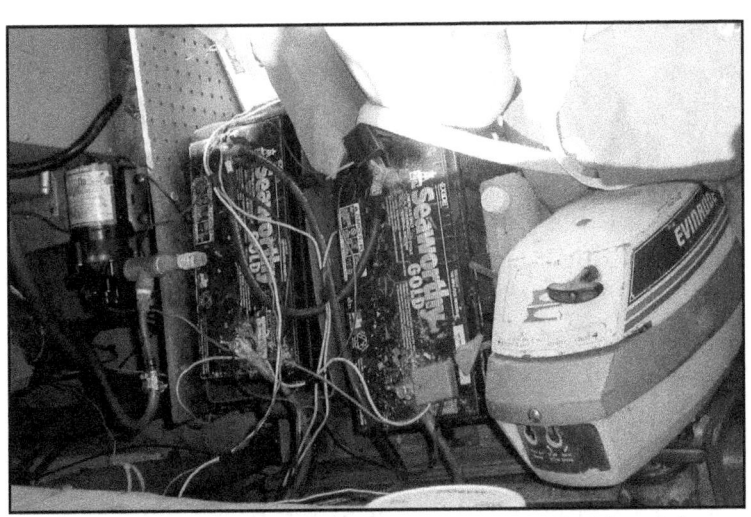

These batteries were not tied to the battery shelf and the battery shelf was not fixed to the boat at all. One sharp heel to port and the batteries would be on the engine.

Skylark's new deck layout is strong and well backed under the deck by the original hardspot and 1/2" HDPE. All the foredeck fittings survived a tow for 23 hours against the Rhine river current from Tiel, NL to Cologne, Germany, with no problem.

advisors made me aware of Optima AGM sealed batteries that could be mounted in any position and are spill-proof. A search on the internet and I found stainless steel trays for racing motorboats with rods and cross bars to hold the batteries in position in the event of a rollover.

One overnight hanging off the old 40lb Danforth anchor well set in the harbor mud, necessitating a break out and handing a 40lb Danforth anchor on board quickly told me that I wanted a windlass. A Lewmar V2 windlass was installed on the conveniently placed "hard spot" in the middle

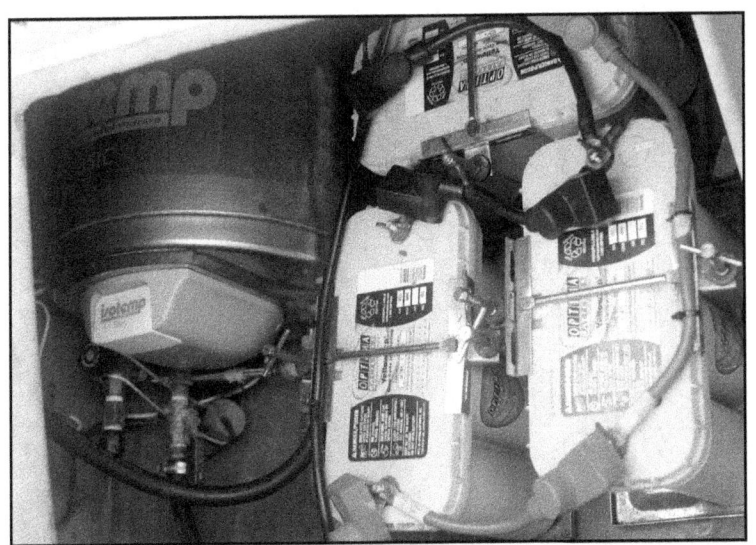

Two pieces of 11-ply 3/4" plywood were epoxied together, racing battery holddowns were installed. Sealed Optima AGM batteries won't leak, even in a rollover.

of the bow where the original single bow cleat had been. I removed the Marinium bow chocks and replaced them with stainless steel chocks several sizes larger and two 12" Herreshoff cleats were mounted on either side of the windlass. 100 feet of 3/8" chain, 200 feet of 12 plait 5/8" anchor line now falls neatly into the forepeak.

I took a chance on a new product and ordered a new-to-the-market Manson Supreme 45lb anchor, one size larger than specified for a 36' boat.

One tip here: I used a 4" hole saw and an old Craftsman 1/2 hp 1/2" drill to cut the hole for the windlass. I drilled a pilot hole and then positioned the small bit of the hole saw and began to cut through the Treadmaster and the fiberglass of

The original foredeck had only one cleat and very small Skene chocks. Not a good arrangement for serious cruising.

the deck. All went well until I cut through the fiberglass. When the 4" hole saw reached the 3/4" plywood of the "hard spot", the hole saw bit into the plywood and stopped, but the good ol' Craftsman continued to turn, taking me with it. I was almost thrown off the boat and had a severe sprain in my wrist. When I later complained to Don, the boatyard owner, he told me I should have run the hole saw backwards, so the teeth didn't bite. Why didn't he tell me that to begin with? It was a couple of years before the pain in my wrist went away.

The winter of 2007, I had to take *Skylark* to Uhlien's Marina in Montauk, Long Island. *Skylark* was too heavy for the old cranes at the boatyard to lift. Uhlien's had a travel lift that could lift

Skylark. In my negotiations with Henry Uhlein, I learned that I would be able to work on *Skylark's* interior and her exterior, but I would not be allowed to paint her bottom. Sounded good to me.

One of the members of my boatyard had a 40 foot motor boat that he lived on every summer while he was renting his house to summer tenants. I knew that he only moved his motor boat a few times a year. I once asked him how he kept his bottom so clean of barnacles and he told me that he used expensive International Micron bottom paint and only painted his bottom every five years.

The first project I tackled with Andy, the electrician, was to remove the 37 year old Wilcox-Crittenden marine bronze seacocks. These seacocks have a tapered cone inside and are massive. All four seacocks were frozen open. I knew the previous owner's poor maintenance habits and was sure that the seacocks hadn't been greased or cleaned since Noah retired.

Inside the hull holding the seacock with a large wrench, I tried to turn it off of the thru-hull. With a lot of force, I was able to spin the whole assembly, but the seacock wouldn't turn off the thru-hull. I asked Andy to turn the wrench and seacock while I went under the boat and tried to hold the thru-hull. No go. I thought I should just take a saber saw and cut out the thru-hulls and cover the hole with fiberglass and cut a new hole and mount a new thru-hull. I called Don, the boatyard owner to discuss my plan. As he often had

The original 40 year old Wilcox-Crittenden naval bronze seacocks cleaned up beautifully and will last longer than me or the boat.

better ideas, having worked in shipyards as a young boy during WWII, I was happy to learn that he had experience with stubborn seacocks. He told me to get a "burr", a carbide rotary file, chuck it into a drill. Then carefully grind the edge of the hole in the thru-hull until I cut around where the flange met the threaded pipe.

    The first thru-hull took me 15 minute to cut the flange away. The flange fell to the ground and Andy inside the boat just lifted the seacock out of the hull. The second thru-hull took 10 minutes and by the time I got to the fourth and smallest seacock, I had it cut out in 5 minutes. I took all four seacocks, 3 were 1-1/2" and one was 3/4", to

Charles Schwendler who worked in a car shop. He put all four seacocks into the auto parts washer and left them soaking overnight. When I returned to his shop in the morning, all four seacocks had been completely disassembled and he told me to take the pieces to a bench grinder with a wire brush attached and polish up the pieces. All the pieces shined up to a nice golden color. I greased them well and reassembled them.

I had looked at new Groco seacocks that were the closest quality to the old Wilcox-Crittenden models. W/C is no longer making seacocks or parts available. Groco's 1-1/2" seacocks list for $229 and have stainless steel balls in the assembly. W/C's are all bronze.

Recently, the installation of seacocks containing brass was allowed in the EU, providing they were changed every five years. Brass can dezincify in a week, I think my bronze seacocks will last my lifetime. Later, when my wife was visiting "the money pit" at the boatyard, I showed her the seacocks. All nice and shiny. I told her that I had had them gold plated for corrosion resistance and I thought she was going to have a heart attack.

Uhlien launched *Skylark* in April 2008 and she returned to the boatyard in East Hampton. I went back home to Cologne, returning in July for more work with my electrician.

Next project was to mount a bow roller. Trying to find one that was long and strong enough was not too difficult, but when my bow roller arrived, I quickly realized that it was not one that I ordered. It surely looked beefy enough though and I held it in place between the now oversized Skene chocks and the chainplate of the forestay. I chose the starboard side of the chainplate to mount it, but I still needed to cut a 1/2" gap in the outward-turning flange on the top of the bow roller to fit it to next to the forestay chainplate. I used 1/4" and 1/2" pieces of HDPE to shim up the bow roller to allow the chain to run in a straight line to the windlass. The chain stopper between the bow roller and the windlass also had to be raised to reach the same plane. The windlass was raised 3/4" off the deck mounted on a piece of Daytona board, the chain stopper had to be raised 1/2" and the bow roller was raised 1/2". Now the chain ran in a level line from the rubber roller to the windlass.

Two Lewmar foot switches were installed behind the windlass and I think the layout I devised for the two Skene chocks, the two Herreshoff 10" cleats, the windlass, chain stopper and bow roller couldn't have been better.

I replaced the old deck cowl that had been used to lead the anchor rode into the anchor locker with a deck plate and installed a hose fitting. With a "T" fitting at the 3/4" Wilcox-Crittenden seacock for the toilet supply, I ran a 3/4" reinforced vinyl hose from that seacock to a pump and then to the hose outlet on deck. Now I could toggle the raw water to the toilet or to the wash-down pump and rinse the anchor chain as it came onboard.

I decided to use 1/2" Staset line for the new halyards and sheets and buying 400 feet in one purchase saved more money. The old Lewmar wire winch for the main halyard was still serviceable, so we installed a new wire halyard.

When we wanted to rewire the mast, I bought some 1" plastic conduit and aluminum pop rivets to make up a conduit in the mast. We removed the mast from the boat and started pulling the old wiring out, only to discover that there was a conduit already installed. I am not sure who built *Skylark's* mast. I think it was Isomat, but whoever built it did a great job. There is a slight taper to the top and the conduit was welded in, but the welding spots on the outside of the mast are hardly visible. I am not a racer, but I don't think it is possible to bend this mast. *Skylark* doesn't have an adjustable backstay anyway.

When it came to replacing the standing rigging, Pearson is known for having oversized stays. The original Navtec turnbuckles had seen better days and the threaded bronze rods that were part of the assembly were pretty corroded. I needed to buy new turnbuckles and have new stays made up.

Rudy the Rigger

The boatyard rigger agreed to let me purchase all the hardware and Defender gave me a trade discount. I paid $80 each for $200 bronze and stainless steel turnbuckles and there were 8 of them. Rudy Ratsep, the rigger, told me to order the stays slightly longer than the originals, have them swaged with an eye at the top of the stay and we would install Sta-Lok fittings at the bottom of each stay. *Skylark's* mast is stepped on the keel and will stand with no stays, this made removing several stays at once easier. We assembled a 50' pipe from 2" PVC pipe and inserted the old stay alongside the new stay so both stays were parallel and stayed clean. One of the Sta-Lok fittings galled the threads upon assembly, but I had ordered a backup cap shroud and an extra Sta-Lok fitting so the rigging was replaced without a hitch.

First Survey

When *Skylark* was surveyed, the surveyor was upset by the water damage in the main cabin that was caused by the silicon failure of the chainplates and the toerail. He emailed me and told me that the water damage and other issues were so bad that I would save some money if he didn't have to write up the survey. I told him to give me the bad news first.

It says right on the tube that silicon is good for 25 years and Skylar was pushing 35. The leaking toerails was a major project and one that I

I can imagine the previous owner was getting overwhelmed by the leaks that plagued the toerails and chainplates. Wet mattresses must have been a constant problem, they certainly were during the crossing.

intended to deal with when I got the boat to Europe and had access to a woodworker's shop.

Skylark's chainplates are not bolted to bulkheads rather they are bolted to massive fiberglass knees that are made by wrapping many layers of fiberglass over a plywood form. I used a space heater to dry the knees and realized that the plywood was just for shape, the fiberglass was so thick, the wood was superfluous. The chainplates were pulled and the 3/4" plywood was dried as much as possible

Cold Beer

Sailing a few times in Holland taught me that ice in cubes or blocks is hard to find in Northern Europe. One can buy small bags of cubesfor high prices at some gas stations, but I couldn't find block ice anywhere. What was I going to do with the original icebox that was designed to use ice for cooling? A visit to a boat show in Düsseldorf led me to discover electric coolers made by Dometic and other companies. These refrigeration systems are self-contained and used for caravans as well as boats. I saw that the models on display could run on 12 volts or 220 volts. I was curious if they would also run on 120 volts. When I contacted a Dometic dealer in the US, where the prices were cheaper, I was told that "No", the US models only ran on 120 volts or 12 volts.

Hmm.

I sent an email to Dometic in Sweden, posing my voltage question and got no response. I called Dometic UK and the nice lady that I spoke to told me that these units ran on 12 volt and 100-240 volts and 50-60 cycles. All I had to do was change the power cord so the plug matched the outlet. I bought the biggest model that Dometic offered. 110 liters. I thought I would install it in the pilot berth that extended under the cockpit.

When I tried to fit the refrigerator lengthwise into the pilot berth, it was too tall to fit without cutting the bulkhead. I decided to mount the refrigerator athwart-ship. My electrician had the brilliant idea of cutting an insert out of the cabinetry under the companionway ladder that was the same shape as one of the refrigerator handles. This allowed the refrigerator to be locked in position on the inboard end and then with a few teak "L"s, we were able to fix the refrigerator in position. A turnbuckle and short cable allow the outboard end of the refrigerator to be held down firmly. I have the coldest beer in northern Europe!

Superwind

To charge the ship's batteries at sea, I had two options. One was to use solar charging, but the output of the panels combined with the fact that Northern Europe is not all that sunny, led me to focus on a wind generator. There are many manufacturers and models to choose from and I was a bit lost. I had visited a huge marina in Porto, Portugal and walked up and down the docks, looking and listening to the various wind generators.

Luckily, I found a Practical Sailor magazine article that reviewed most of the wind generators on the market. The Superwind 350 caught my attention. It was the most powerful, but the most expensive. Practical Sailor gave the unit some bad comments, such as the company was new and no one knew how long they would be in business, plus from an American point of view, the factory was in Germany and repairs and replacements might be problematic. When I learned that the factory was 15 minutes from my home in Cologne, Germany, I was sold. I visited the factory and asked Klaus Krieger, the president if he had any "demo" models or refurbished models. He told methat there were very few that ever needed repair and those he donated to various expeditions. He told me to contact his US distributor. I did and got a $100 discount. The US distributor also gave me a contact for a supplier of a mast to hold the wind generator.

The Superwind 350 was rated by Practical Sailor as the most powerful wind generator tested, also the most expensive and the drawback to them was that the factory was in Germany and turned out to be 20 minutes from my house. That was the deal clincher. This is also the quietest generator, I have to look at it to see if it running.

Since I also had to mount the Raymarine radome, I had the idea of combining the radome and the wind generator on one mast that I would mount on the stern. I didn't like the idea of attaching the radome to the ship's mast for several reasons. I had a beautiful radar mast delivered with a shelf to mount the radome. I did have some minor problems fitting the wind generator to the mast as the bushing at the bottom of the wind generator was in millimeters and the mast was US pipe sizes. Also, when I surveyed my intended mounting location at the stern, I realized the the deck was only about 3/8" of an inch thick with no core. I knew I would have to "beef up" that spot.

I also had to mount two large "tangs" to fix the Jordan series drogue to the stern. I didn't want to use the stern cleats for that purpose, so I added layer upon layer of fiberglass cloth to the underside of both the port and starboard corners of the aft deck. Working within the aft lazarette was a real job and I wound up with globs of epoxy and thickener in my hair.

The winter of 2008, I didn't want to leave the boat at Uhlien's and my best option was to berth the boat at one of the fancier marinas near the boatyard. The marina I chose had a bubbling system that would, in theory, prevent ice from forming around the boat. I had some extra money and decided that I wanted to have *Skylark* shrink-wrapped. I thought that I left *Skylark* well-snugged for the winter and even left a small ceramic heater

This wonderful multivoltage battery charger from ProMariner charges up to three banks and only requires changing the plug on the shore power. The voltage changes automatically. The company gives great service. Somehow, this secure location away from rain or spray got wet and ProMariner replaced the whole unit without a question.

running near the engine with the thermostat set to kick the heater on above 32°F.

I was surprised when I returned in March of 2009, boarded *Skylark* and went into the cabin. I first noticed that there were no cabin lights.

I realized that the battery charger wasn't charging. Either someone had unplugged the shore power or *Skylark's* heater and battery charger had combined to trip the circuit breaker on the shore power and no one reset the circuit breaker.

I realized that the battery charger wasn't charging. Either someone had unplugged the shore power or *Skylark's* heater and battery charger had combined to trip the circuit breaker on the shore power and no one reset the circuit breaker.

The bilge was full of water to 2 inches below the cabin sole. All the mast wiring was under water! Thanks to the high quality Pacer Marine electrical connectors and the ProMarine battery charger, once I reconnected the shore power, the charger came online and charged the five Optima AGM Series 31 Yellow Top batteries.

All the circuits on the mast functioned. I opened the connectors, squirted some WD-40 in them and haven't had any problems with those connections since.

Eventually, I replaced the Raymarine wind instrument junction box that wasn't watertight with a AquaSignal five conductor waterproof connection.

Now when stepping the mast, I don't have to unscrew and separate those five small gauge wires.

Just plug and play.

Trip Planning

When *Skylark* was purchased in 2007, I started planning the route across the Atlantic that would be the easiest on the boat and on the crew.

Much reading of various Atlantic Crossing guides, tales by Eric Forsyth, the sailing explorer, National Geographic, anything related to the North Atlantic was interesting. When I wasn't sourcing supplies, I was reading how the mating season for the Right whales was May and June south of Nova Scotia, directly in the path of our great circle route to Ireland.

Great!

So now, not only did I have to worry about fog, icebergs, container ships, I had to worry about mating whales not paying attention to a little sailboat sliding silently through the fog.

After two summers of projects, *Skylark* was nearly ready for her transAtlantic crossing. One of the final items needed was a life-raft. I am a coastal sailor and never felt the necessity for a life-raft, but crossing an ocean was different. I looked into buying a life-raft, but the good ones were expensive and the cheap ones were not much more than a wading pool for children. I looked into renting a life-raft, but the monthly rental, combined with the return shipping wasn't cheap either.

Charles Schwendler, one of my advisors had visited the Newport, RI boat show and had "won" a gift certificate of a 30% price reduction on a Givens life-raft. I looked at the Givens website and was shocked by the highest prices of all the raft companies. Givens did have a video documentation of US Coast Guard tests that showed how effective their rafts were in high winds. Still, the price for a 6 man offshore model was close to $7000. With Charles' discount, the price was still around $5000.

Planet Claire

While I was pondering a solution, I received a phone call from the manager of the B-52's rock group. I had made photos of the group back in the 70s and one of those photos was used as their first album cover. Since I had made these photos on my own, I owned all the rights. It seemed that the group wanted to use the original album cover photo for t-shirts.

Manna from heaven...I asked for $5000 and the group agreed. The Givens six man offshore deluxe model is now called "Planet Claire" and I hope I never have to go there.

In November 2008, I paid Givens in full for the life-raft and told the company that I needed the raft the following April.

Since 2007 when I bought *Skylark,* the whole reason for the purchase was to get her over to The Netherlands. I had sailed with German Captain Michael Zapf on a chartered sail training weekend. Some of my wife's friends were working on getting their German sailing licenses and none of them actually owned a boat or knew someone that would lend them a boat. This, plus the fact that for the Germans to collect hours at the helm for their required license upgrades, they had to keep a personal log book and have an instructor sign off on their hours.

When I joined Captain Mike for a weekend charter, I ponyed up the €250 euros that each person paid and went along for the ride.

Since all of the others were there to collect their hours, they were constantly trying to get the helmsman's spot. Captain Mike asked me once as I was lolling on a berth in the salon if I would like a turn at the helm.

I told him that I have my own boat in the US and that I am the one who has to take the helm when the weather goes sour and no one else wants to be on deck. I get plenty of sailing time, especially in foul weather. I said that the weather was too nice for me to take the helm.

None of my pals in the boatyard had time or were interested in making an Atlantic crossing. I knew that The Mate, a veteran of many summer cruises in New England and a great hand at splicing and whipping, would want to make the trip. He always tried to detour the summer cruise to Bermuda, but my Pearson 26 didn't have the water storage capacity or the fuel capacity to make such a long offshore voyage without major modifications. I called him about the transAtlantic he signed on immediately. Later, he told me that his wife had put the kibosh on the idea. She thought I was crazy. I knew that the Mate didn't have the financial resources to cover his airplane tickets or food for the trip, so I offered to loan him the necessary money. His wife made him take a "Safety at Sea" course, he bought a deep sea diver's suit for his foul weather gear and he bought a "new to the market" SPOT device (more about this later).

I also contacted Dominic Dreyfus, a British sailor and good friend of many years, who jumped at the chance as well. He volunteered to be the ship's cook and started working up store's lists and menus.

By now, the plans were falling into place. In late April of 2009, I returned to Long Island and looked at the remaining projects to complete. Install the Gasgone oven, the propane system, calibrate the Raymarine electronics, fit larger teak pieces next to the companionway, install beefier hand rails on the deck and on the overhead in the cabin, finish the wiring for the wind generator, change the 35 amp stock alternator on the Yanmar to a 70 amp Balmar, add engine water heating to the water heater. I had the Mate go over the seams of the toe rail and ports with silicone as a temporary fix. I knew that I would be changing the toe rails and reglazing the ports at a later date in Europe.

As far as the Mate's splicing skills, I had 100 feet of 3/8" chain that I wanted to splice together with 3/4" 12-plait line. The Mate never met 12-plait line, but reading instructions from an internet article, he gave it a "go", decided that it wasn't right and spliced it again, getting it right.

He fixed the bitter end of the 300 foot rode with some small stuff to a ring bolt we mounted in the anchor locker. We connected the 45lb Manson Supreme anchor to the other end with a stainless steel swivel and brought the rode into the anchor locker with the windlass. The small stuff on the bitter end was several loops of 1/8" nylon line that would allow us to quickly cut the rode, in case of emergency and we had to drop the anchor. Cutting through 3/4" line would take more time and a very sharp knife.

As word started to get out of my impending doom, Rick Doherty, a college friend visited the boatyard to check on the final stages of the project. By now, I had a team of 4-6 people working from dawn to dusk, adding backing plates, covering cockpit speaker holes, removing old cowls used for ventilating the old gasoline engine and replacing them with deck plates. A funny point was that when we installed the oven with gimbals, there was so much teak, paint and other supplies stored in the V-berth that we would be carrying to Europe, when *Skylark* finally arrived in Europe and all that material was removed from the V-berth, the oven was way off level. During the crossing, we even had to shift a lot of material from the V-berth, as *Skylark* was too bow heavy.

She would carry 20 gallons of extra fuel in diesel cans stored in the cockpit. I bought two 26

George, the captain, The Mate and Andy, the electrician posing for the East Hampton newspaper.

gallon flexible water tanks, fitted them with valves and long hoses to be able to transfer the water to the built-in tanks. I stored one flexible tank in the pilot berth behind the refrigerator and one in a compartment under the V-berth, both spaces were lined with carpeting to avoid chafing the flexible tanks. After filling all the tanks, we would have 96 gallons of water to cross the ocean.

Not that much and as it turned out, not enough.

Jerry Hodgens, was a Marine officer in Vietnam. Jerry had been a captain in the New York City Fire Department, a crewman on an ocean-going tug making several Atlantic crossings. He had even been in a Marion, CT/Bermuda race on a wooden Alden cutter. Returning to New York on the Alden, they got hit by a hurricane in the Gulf

Stream, the boat fell apart under them, popping fasteners and planks, seams opening, the worst nightmare.

Fortunately, they were able to get a Mayday off and were picked up by a Russian freighter. The point being that this guy had a lot of blue water experience and as I got closer to the actual departure for Europe, Jerry began to take my project seriously and started to give me tips.

Even though we had the Dometic refrigerator on board, he suggested getting thick-walled styrofoam containers, pre-freezing our meats and other freezable foods and storing these foods with dry ice. He said that a cooler prepared this way, would keep the food frozen for more than a week.

I asked him about washing ourselves during the crossing and he just laughed. Don't wash and waste fresh water. The ocean will be too cold on the northern route. Just take baby buttwipes and clean ourselves with those.

He told me about the official Pilot Charts of the North Atlantic. These are not charts for navigation, rather for time of year route planning. The book of pilot charts is quite a large format and are designed with over 100 years of collected samples. Averages for each month showing wind directions and strength, monthly average of the percentage of gales, the ocean currents at different times of the year and what was particularly interesting to me; the most southern reach of icebergs, with the year of discovery.

Stirring up a bit of local interest, we had a visit from a reporter from one of the East Hampton newspapers. I was the first "member" of my boatyard who would ever sail from the boatyard to Europe. The advice was starting to come in thick and heavy the closer we got to our departure date. The life-raft which had been ordered months in advance wasn't ready and my choice was now down to borrowing an out-of-date Givens from a sister-ship owner or waiting until the life-raft was completed and picking it up in Rhode Island on our way. The crew decided to wait a week or two more. Givens has since gone out of business due to bad management.

On May 28, 2009, after spending over $700 on food alone, we boarded *Skylark*. With quite a few unfinished minor projects, we filled the fixed and the flexible water tanks, slipped our lines and left East Hampton, NY bound for Newport to pickup the Givens. The crew was the Mate, my college friend Rick and Andy, who volunteered to go as far as St. John's, Newfoundland.

Tragically, Dominic Dreyfus, my English pal who was to be the cook, had his oldest son die in a tragic bicycle accident on the Via de la Muerte in Peru just a few weeks before our departure and obviously couldn't make the trip.

Ben Morris, another English sailor was going to meet us in St. John's, where Rick and Andy would leave the ship. Ben was bringing an Iridium phone and a sextant.

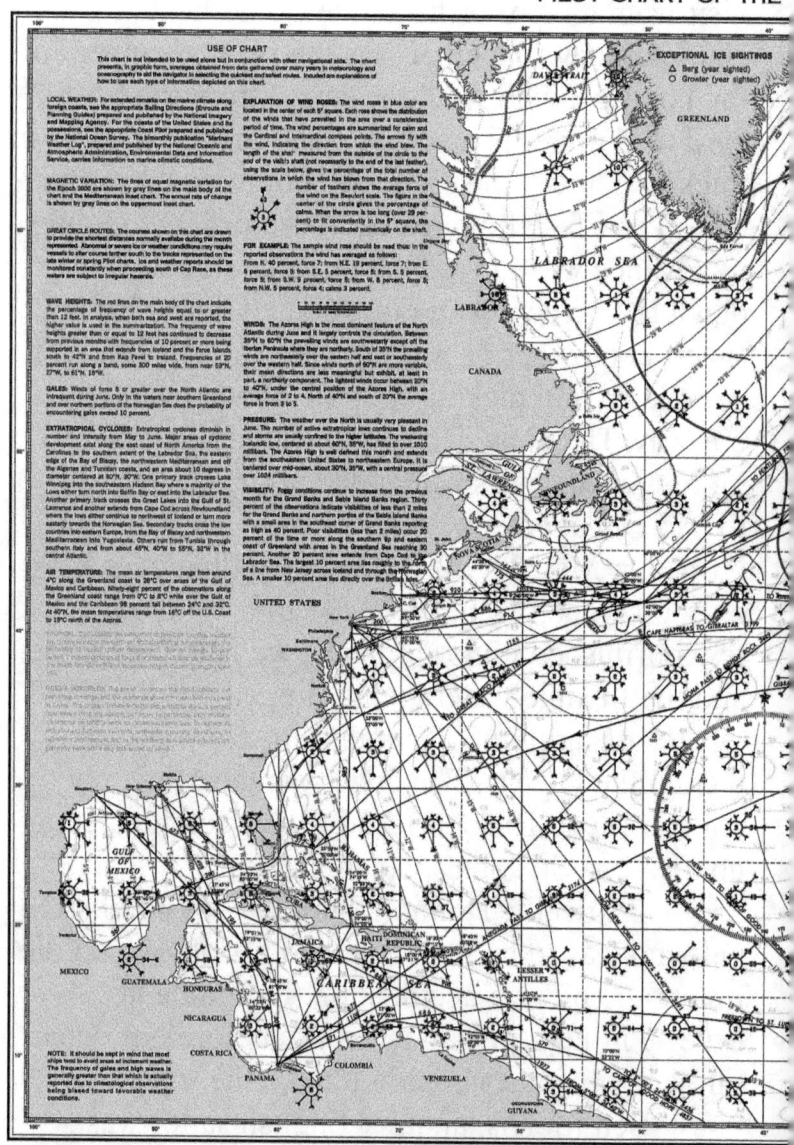

Pilot charts are tools for route planning and show the average wind directions and gale frequency for all twelve months of the year. Detailed instructions for use

NORTH ATLANTIC OCEAN

SEC. I - JUNE

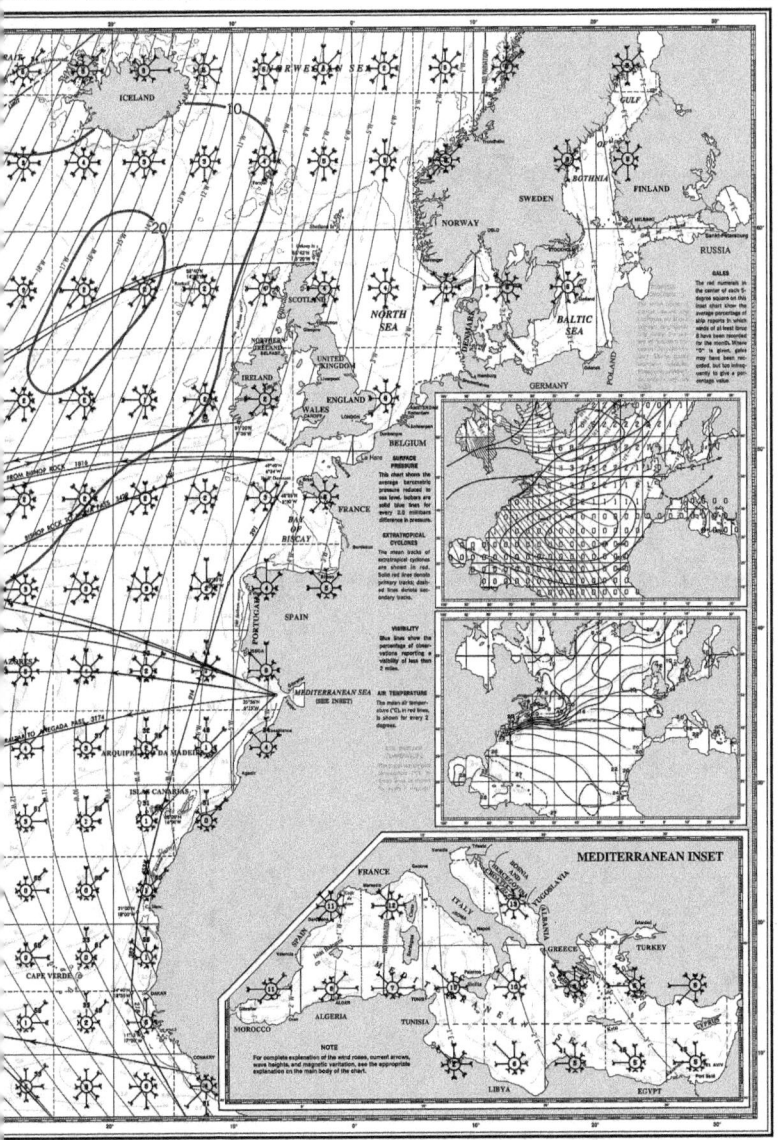

are printed on each page. Great Circle routes, history of known iceberg positions, major currents and monthly averages for barometric pressure are shown in colors.

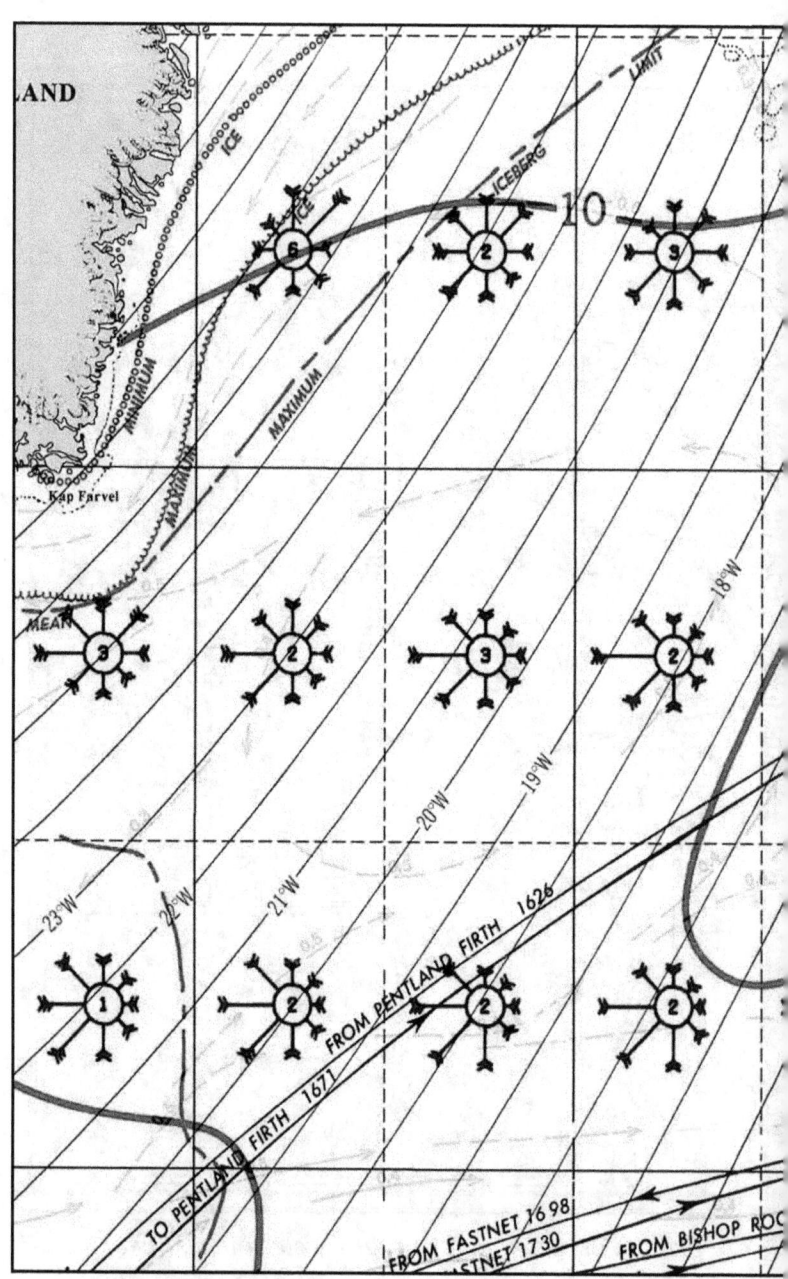

The wind roses show the average percentage of gales during each month. The arrows show the averages

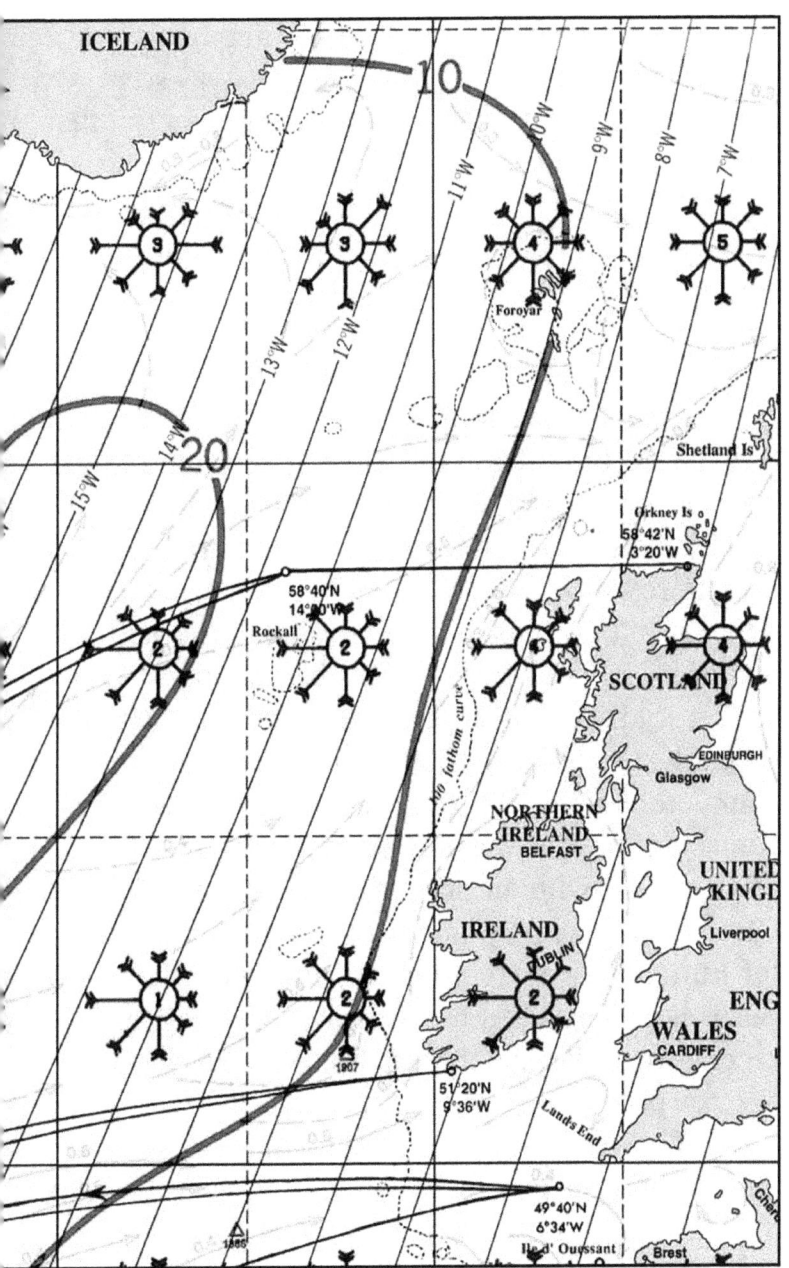

of the wind strength and the direction it comes from.

As soon as we left the slip at the boatyard, we ran aground on a sandbar. *Skylark* was so loaded with supplies and construction material that her water line must have been 6" lower.

We wiggled our way through the slimy mud of the sand bar and found the channel out of the harbor.

What's a Zarpe?

We basically motored from East Hampton to Newport, RI to pickup the life-raft. I wanted to get a zarpe in Newport, as it was the last official port of entry to the US that we would land in. During my trip research, I realized the word "zarpe" doesn't exist in the Coast Guard vocabulary and after numerous calls to Coast Guard bases, one kind officer told me that the closest document the Coast Guard has was Form 1300, a clearance paper for commercial ships. I prepared several copies and contacted the Customs office and made an appointment with an officer for 0100 the following morning. I just wanted to start my paper trail for Europe in a correct fashion and knew that Europeans, Germans in particular, love papers, especially with nice blue stamps of authority. I got my "zarpe".

Thursday, May 30th, found *Skylark* and crew bound for Provincetown, MA. our last port in the US. Reaching P'town, I was shocked a the high prices for a slip at the Provincetown Marina. It was $3 a foot, up at least 100% since the last

My cousin, Pierre G.T. Beauregard V came to serenade us with his masterful harmonica playing. P'town rocks...

Rick, my college pal, Andy, the electrician and the captain waiting for the Givens liferaft to be finished.

time I had visited that artist colony! We met my cousin, Pierre Beauregard, who serenaded us for hours with his harmonica playing. My college pal, Rick, came to me with the bad news that he was returning to Philadelphia, his mother just had a stroke and he had to get back to her. That left *Skylark* with me, the Mate and the electrician, Andy.

Not wishing to linger in P'town, we left the following noon for Lunenburg, Canada. As we rounded Race Point, the northern tip of Cape Cod and set a northeast course for Nova Scotia, large whales treated us to a sight while they were feeding off Race Point. We had full sails set for Canada.

That evening the wind gradually veered to the northwest and began to increase. By midnight, it was blowing over 35 knots and *Skylark* was struggling under the full main and #2 genoa. I called for the Mate to come on deck, take the wheel and head us upwind so I could drop the main sail. The Mate told me it was too windy to point the boat up. I couldn't be at the mast to lower the sail and at the wheel. I released the main halyard and pulled down on the luff. I heard a pop and then more pops as I realized that the sail slides were breaking away from the new mainsail. Then the sail was down. I tied some sail ties around the furled main and went back to the cockpit to scowl at The Mate. Obviously, he had been away from the sea too long and had forgotten how to sail. At least, if I could find sail slides in Canada, the Mate would be deligated to sew them on.

We had loaded four 5 gallon cans of diesel in the cockpit for extra fuel. *Skylark's* permanent tank held only 20 gallons and not that I was intending to motor to Europe, extra fuel would always be good to have. On top of the four diesel cans that were tied together, we placed the Givens and on top of that we placed the Jordan series drogue. I thought that the first emergency item we might need would be the drogue and if that didn't work, we would have easy access to the life-raft. Unfortunately, I hadn't tied the fuel cans to the pad-eyes in the cockpit, I hadn't tied the life-raft to the pad-eyes and I hadn't tied the Jordan to the pad-eyes. They all were stacked up in the cockpit and made a comfortable seat for the helmsman, but they weren't tied to anything.

June 1st found *Skylark,* under clear blue skies crossing the Gulf of Maine with winds gusting to 40 knots and 2-3 meter waves. The wind coming from the northwest, I was alone at the helm and we were reaching along nicely under the #2 genoa alone, heading directly for Lunenberg. Suddenly, a wave from a more northerly direction slammed the side of the boat. I ducked down at the helm to avoid getting soaked. When I stood up, I noticed that the Jordan series drogue was lying on the starboard lazarette hatch.

How did that get there, I thought?

After our near disaster and almost losing the Givens overboard, we connected the bridle of the drogue to its massive tangs and tied the Givens to the pad-eyes. The captain should have been flogged for not securing this important gear.

    I turned around and saw that the fuel tanks were still with us, but the Givens was gone. As I looked over the stern, I saw the Givens riding up the face of a wave 100 feet behind us. I called "All hands on deck" and the Mate and electrician woke upand came on deck.

    I started the engine and spun the boat around, telling The Mate to keep his eye on the Givens. Within two minutes, we were alongside the raft and I recall being so pumped with adrenaline that I just leaned over the side and snatched the Givens out of the water, passing it to the crew.

    I was stupid not to have tied the raft, the

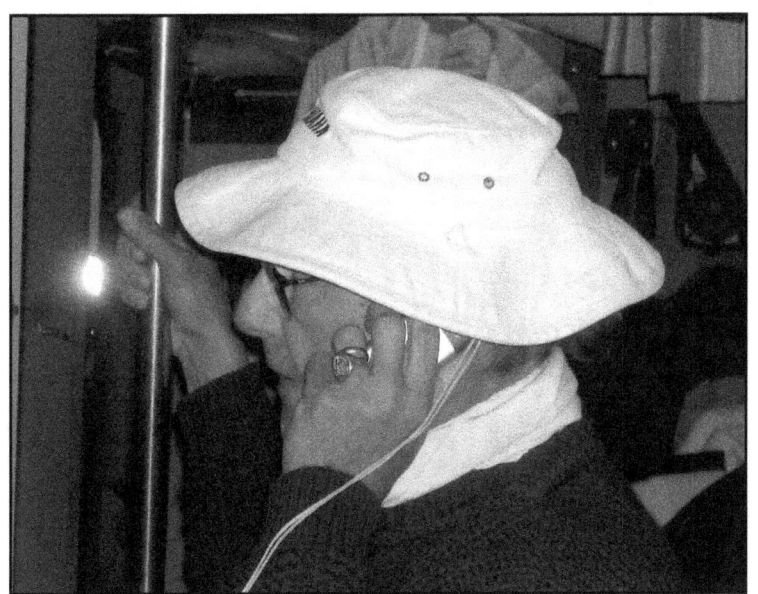

*The captain reporting Skylark's arrival in Canada.
"No Ma'am, we have no guns, only knives."*

drogue and fuel cans to the pad-eyes. I should have had the painter for the Givens prefixed to a cleat. Lucky for me I am stupid sometimes, if I had tied the painter to the boat and this mishap had occurred, we would have been dealing with an inflated raft in the middle of a near-gale. We tied the life-raft and drogue on top of the fuel cans, then everything to padeyes and resumed our sail to Lunenberg.

    Arriving at Lunenberg around 9pm, it was getting dark. We motored into the harbor looking for a place to tie up. Lunenberg is famous for building ships for hundreds of years. *Bluenose*, the famous Canadian racing schooner, was in port undergoing a refit. We docked by the museum. I

Lunenberg, Nova Scotia is the home of "Bluenose" the famous racing schooner. She was actually there for renovations.

Lunenberg's museum was closed during our night stopover.

called the Canadian immigration and reported our arrival. I was asked if we had any weapons on board and reported we only had knives. If we had had a gun, we would have had to declare it, leave it at our port of entry and then return to pick up the weapon upon leaving Canada. Since we didn't intend to leave Canada until we reached St. John's, NF, returning to Lunenberg would have been most inconvenient.

The crew found a nice pub and had a good meal. We learned that the Canadian dollar was called a "Loonie" and the Canadian two dollar coin was called a "Toonie". The following morning, we decided to leave for Halifax in hopes of finding sail slides to replace the broken ones from the previous evening's gale and even better, an authorized Raymarine technician to have a look at our malfunctioning autopilot. Prior to leaving East Hampton, one of our last chores was to calibrate the fluxgate compass and the autopilot. The compass didn't present any problems, but the autopilot didn't seem to be able to hold a course for more than 15 minutes.

When we arrived at Halifax and motored up the long harbor to the Dartmouth Yacht Club, we found a berth and the first thing I did was call Raymarine in the US. They put me onto a commercial ships' electronics firm and the company agreed to send us a technician the following afternoon. The next morning, I headed off to a chandlery and bought some sail slides. The slides available were either too narrow for *Skylark's* mainsail mast track or they were too wide. I bought the wide ones with the idea of sanding them narrower to fit the track.

That evening we stopped at the yacht club's bar for a nightcap and struck up a conversation with some of the members. "Where were we from?" and "Where were we going?" led to a discussion of our broken sail slides. One of the members was the manager of the Doyle sail loft in Halifax. He assured me that if I stopped by his loft in the morning, he would give me some slides with the correct dimensions.

At this point, Andy, the electrician, having suffered from seasickness for three days, decided to jump ship and not continue to St. John's. I had already bought him a plane ticket from St. Johns, so I gave him $100 and told him to take a bus back to New York. I haven't heard from him since.

The Mate and I carried on alone from Halifax to St. Pierre, France. Originally, we had intended to pass through the Bras d'Or lakes, but due to the extra time waiting for the life-raft, we were behind schedule and had a date to meet Ben Morris in St. John's.

We motored along the south coast of Nova Scotia in a light fog. Occasionally we would see the distant shore line and kept a close watch for mating whales. We wanted to stop at a harbor along the way to pickup more fuel, milk for coffee and tobacco.

The bank that ate my ATM bard

Cansco, a harbor at the east end of Nova Scotia looked like a substantial port and we decided to stop there. Cansco was once a major fishing harbor, but now was long past it's heyday. There was no marina, only industrial fishing docks. We tied up and I asked some fishermen loading their boat where I could find fuel.

"Only by an appointment with a fuel truck." was the answer.

I didn't think a truck would be interested in selling 20 gallons, so I headed for a bank to get some cash to do a little shopping.

I found a Canadian bank with a cash machine and when I inserted my ATM card to make a withdrawal, the machine said "Contact your bank." and swallowed my card. It was a Saturday and the bank was going to be closed until Monday. I called my bank in South Carolina only to be told that my card had been put on hold due to the unusual occurrences of "foreign land" withdrawals. The Mate and I pooled our meager cash resources and with the euros, the loonies and a few US dollars, I went to the grocery/hardware store. I asked the manager if he would accept the combination of currencies for a small purchase. He agreed.

With all but the fuel replenished, we headed for St. Pierre.

On June 9th, *Skylark* reached St. Pierre and went to the Douane dock to contact customs and immigration. Although we had reported our entry to Canada in Lunenberg, St. Pierre and its sister island, Miquelon are French colonies. The French tricolor is flown and one has to spend euros on the islands. Since it was 7pm, the offices of the immigration and customs offices were closed.

I called the phone number posted on the door and was told that the immigration officer was at the airport waiting for a plane and would arrive to clear us in later in the evening. When the officer arrived, I showed him our passports, our ship's papers and our zarpe from the US. I had no paper from the entry in Canada. All was friendly and I told the officer we would be staying a few days.

I called Ben Morris's wife in London, to learn that he was flying to St. John's and she would have him call us when he arrived. I asked Ben if he could take a $99 flight from St. John's to St. Pierre, we had to make some repairs and St. John's was at least a two day sail from St. Pierre. I had planned to re-provision in St. John's, but St. Pierre had a large supermarket and a good chandlery so there was no real need of us to go to St. John's.

Ben arrived the following day and immediately set to making some of our repairs. I had only met this Englishman once before in London, but I knew he was a capable sailor, often soloing between his harbor near London and Baltimore, Ireland, where he had a summer cottage. Our spinnaker pole had frozen end fittings, the old stainless vs aluminum story. Ben sawed off a short piece of the spinnaker pole. That gave him access to inside the frozen fitting. Disassembly, WD40 and some sandpaper soon put the spinnaker pole back into operation. I had a spinnaker for *Skylark* on board, but I had never flown one myself. Ben cobbled together some extra lines and blocks and soon had the lines needed for flying the chute.

On the way to St. Pierre, The Mate had reported "hitting" something during the night and although we had no problems or leaks, I was curious about the state of my bottom, prop and rudder.

One morning, we were reeving a flag halyard, I saw a inflatable come into the St. Pierre Yacht Club, where we were tied up. There were two divers in the boat. I quickly caught up with one of the divers on the dock still in his wetsuit and asked him if he would dive under *Skylark* and have a look for any damage. He agreed and after he came up from under the boat, he told us that the keel was still there with no damage. The prop and rudder looked fine, but there was no ball zinc on the propeller shaft.

Hmm. We had hit something and now the zinc was gone. A trip to the chandlery produced no shaft zinc that would fit my 7/8" prop shaft. I have since learned that 7/8" prop shafts are not very common and now have a stock of 7/8" zincs.

During our motor over from Cansco to St. Pierre, The Mate noticed that one of the two support poles for the radar/wind generator mast had

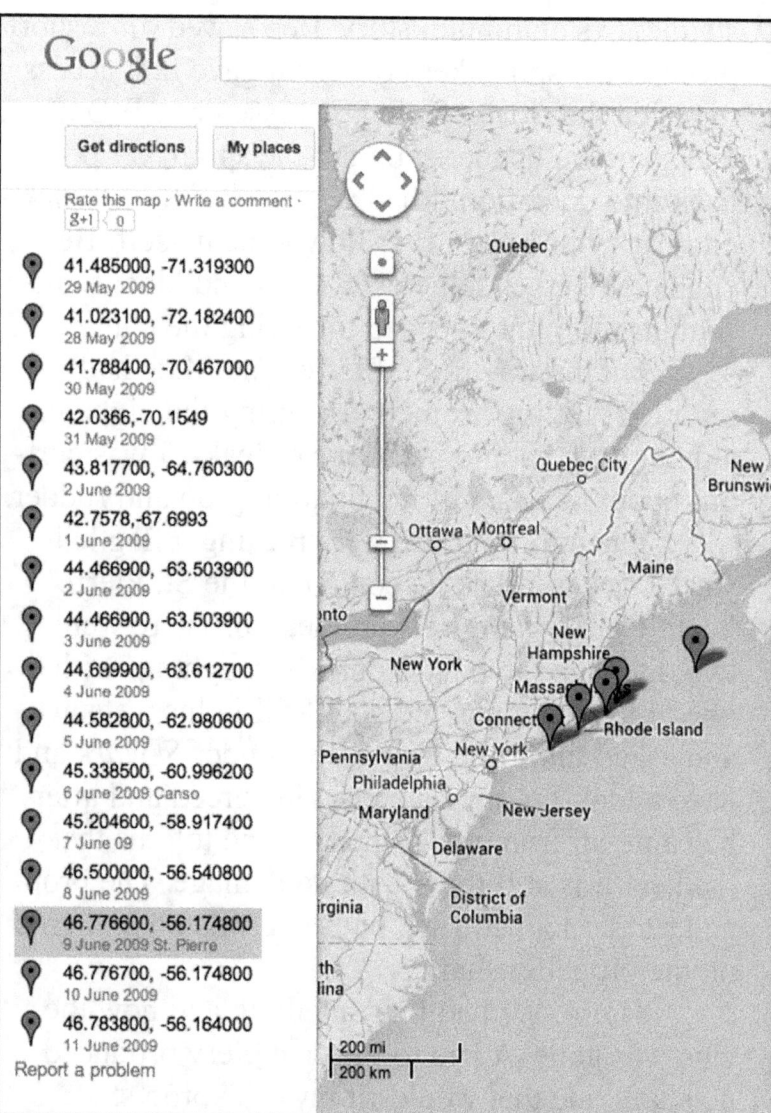

This is a GoogleEarth map record of the daily position reporting by an "at the time" new technology called "SPOT". The Mate's neurotic wife insisted that he use this device inspite of the fact that there was a new and registered EPIRB on board Skylark.

The Mate's twin brother in Ohio kept a daily

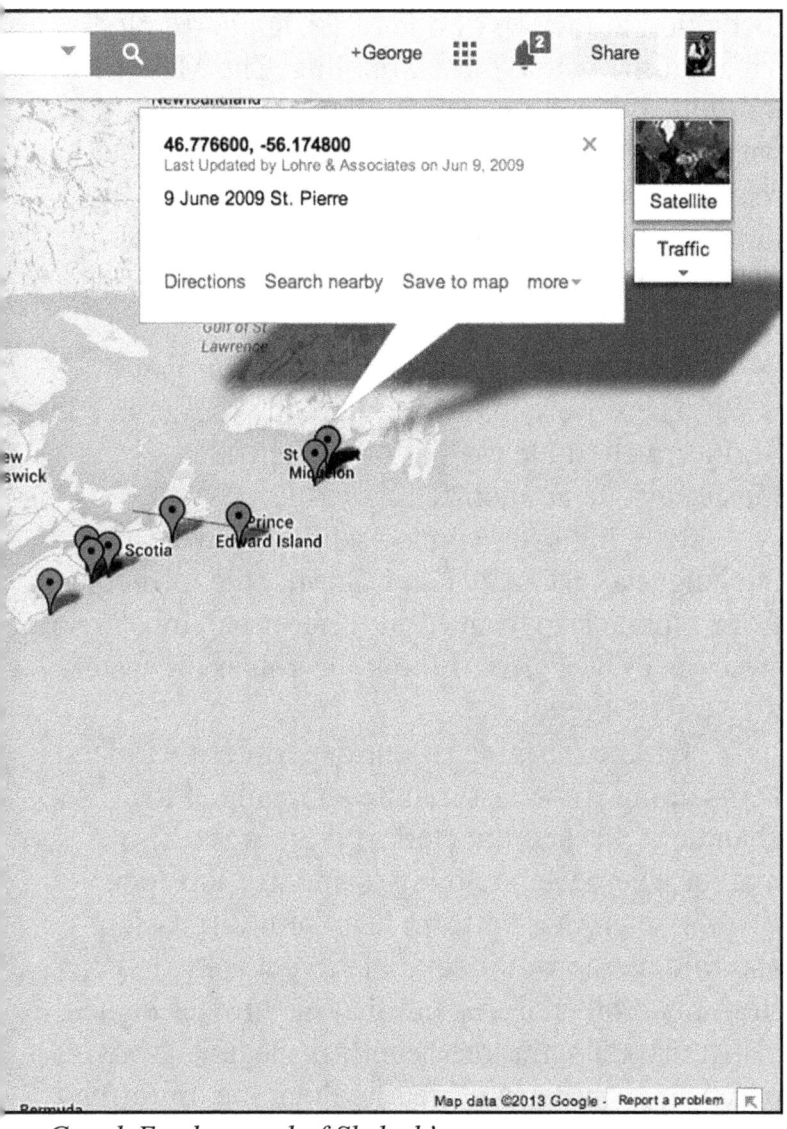

GoogleEarth record of Skylark's progress.

As captain, I had no business allowing this device on board, especially when The Mate didn't have full understanding of its functions.

Operating manuals are made to be read.

lost a bolt at the top of one of the support poles. This left the whole mast wobbling. The Mate tied up the mast to the stern rail, but I didn't think that was going to work across the Atlantic. We replaced the missing bolt, added double locking nuts to all the other bolts and for belts and suspenders, we added some long hose clamps around the mast and the stern rail.

We also topped off our fuel and propane...

There were many good French restaurants in St. Pierre and I ate my fill of lobster salad, lobster bisque and lobster casserole.

I am a lobster connoisseur and have eaten the langusta in Jamaica and Florida, the lobsters from Montauk to Maine, but I never had lobster so sweet as in St. Pierre. I think the colder the water, the sweeter the lobster.

On the morning of our departure for Ireland, I was doing some last minute shopping at the chandlery. I asked the clerk if there was a fish market where we could buy some live lobsters.

A man in a uniform heard our discussion and told me he would take me to get some lobster from his brother. Turns out that his brother owned a fish market and three beautiful specimens were purchase for €6 each. I learned that the uniformed gentleman was the chief of police for the island. He even gave me a ride back to the yacht club.

Thursday, June 11th, we had nothing further to do than leave.

It took us a day and a half to reach the

Southwest corner of Newfoundland called Cape Race. The southern shore of Newfoundland is high cliffs and no beaches. We were tacking into shore and then out again.

Always monitor Channel 16

Around 4pm under a strong south wind and cloudy skies, I noticed a black twin engine plane with yellow stripes on the wings flying over us.

What a pretty plane I thought.

When the plane circle around and headed directly toward us, I knew something was up. I wanted to point at our US flag, but realized that the flag was GONE!

The pole must have jumped out of its holder. Where I had no idea.

I yelled into the cabin and asked Ben to turn on the VHF and talk to that plane. We should have had the VHF monitoring channel 16 all the time anyway. Ben spoke to the plane, who patched us through to the Canadian Coast Guard in Halifax.

It turned out that the Canadian Coast Guard had been searching for us since noon!

The SPOT

Now about that SPOT device that The Mate had brought along...

Skylark had a brand new correctly registered EPIRB in our ditch bag. The Mate's wife after realizing she couldn't stop her husband from fulfilling his life's ambition, insisting that he take the

"Safety at Sea" course, buy the deep sea diver's suit and demanded that he buy this new contraption called "SPOT".

This electronic device is essentially a GPS with the capability of transmitting the position of the device to a satellite. Once the satellite receives the signal from the SPOT, it sends a signal to a terrestrial base that sends out an email to a predetermined list of 10 email addresses.

There are three buttons on the device. Button number "1", sends a prepared text message, "We are OK and we are here." giving the latitude and longitude. Button number "2" sends the message "We are NOT OK and we are here." The message doesn't say what is NOT OK. One could be out of fuel, out of beer, whatever. Button number "3" says, "We are here and we need HELP".

Well, around noon on June 12th, The Mate who had assumed duties as communications officer, downloading weather reports and graphics, sending and receiving emails, using the SPOT device to send OK signals with our position so our families and friends could follow our progress on Google Earth, decided that since it was cloudy, the Iridium phone wasn't going to be able to send and receive emails. So he pushed button number 2 thinking that would mean that our families would not be getting an email from us. The Mate didn't read the manual for the SPOT.

When his twin brother sitting in his office

in Cincinnati, Ohio, received the "We are NOT OK and we are here." message, and took a look with Google Earth at the SPOT reported position, he saw that the latitude/longitude position put us right on the rocks of the south coast of Newfoundland.

The twin brother called the Canadian Coast Guard. The Coast Guard officer in Halifax took the call and after listening to the twin, the officer said that he had no reports or EPIRB signals from any ships in that location. How did the twin know that his brother was in trouble. The twin explained that he had the "Help" message from the SPOT device and from the location given, *Skylark* was on the rocks near Cape Race. The officer explained that a search and rescue operation costs upwards of 125,000.00 loonies.

The twin said, "Do a search!"

Luckily for us, the SPOT device was so new to the market that the Canadian Coast Guard had never heard of such a thing. We weren't going to be charged with a false EPIRB signal. But in the meantime, my wife and all the rest of the SPOT message recipients had been receiving the back and forth emails between the twin and the Canadians.

Under the Doghouse

My German wife was furious. She had been against the renovation of an old US boat. She had been against me being away for almost three months that the final renovation and crossing was taking. She was sure that SHE was going to have to personally cover the 125,000.00 Canadian dollars that the search and rescue operation cost.

She didn't communicate with me until I reached The Netherlands a month later. She was still mad four years later.

No bill has ever arrived.

I was ready to keel haul The Mate.

OK, he was a scatterbrained artist, who never had a pot to piss in.

OK. That I had to go against his wife's wishes and loan him the money for his airfares, feed and water him so he could live his life-long dream, but not being aware of the operation of a non-essential piece of equipment that caused an unnecessary search operation was unforgivable. I was the captain. I was responsible for the safety of the crew, the ship and liable for any misuse or mistakes. Luckily there was no cat o' nine tails on board.

Jerry, one of my advisors in the boatyard had given me a lot of tips in the years preceding this voyage. He suggested that I take the northern route across the Atlantic, since my tankage was so limited. He told me that we wouldn't be taking showers in order to conserve water. He suggested baby butt wipes to keep the toe cheese at bay. He told me about the North Atlantic pilot charts that would show me wind direction and strength, the direction of the currents and the southern limits of the icebergs at different months of the year. He told me that we would be cold, cold, cold until we left the Labrador current.

Boy! Was he right! I knew that the predicted water temperature would be 8°C and although we didn't have a water thermometer, the air temperature was also 8°C. It was cold!

The autopilot had developed deeper problems and was refusing to hold a course for more than five minutes. We had to hand steer for our 4 hour watches. Sometimes locking the helm and balancing the sails would get us 30 minutes of self-steering before we would have to reset the sails or adjust the helm.

The first few days after leaving North American, we were on constant lookout for icebergs and ships. Didn't see either.

We were afraid to use the Cozy Cabin heater. We didn't know its rate of propane consumption and wanted to save the propane for cooking. While we all had diver suits or appropriate foul weather gear, only our hands got wet and cold. None of us had satisfactory waterproof gloves, only The Mate had US Army surplus leather gloves. Although the wool liners got wet, they were still warmer than nothing. We would run the engine and hang our gloves on the handle of the refrigerator that protruded into the engine compartment. It was pretty miserable. When not standing watch, eating or cooking, we were in our sleeping bags.

Although we had added a temporary bead of silicone around the toe rails in St. Pierre, the 35 year old silicone from the original toe rail installation had long disappeared. Both the toe rails were leaking through their mounting screw holes and water was streaming down the hull liner. Although we didn't know it, water was building up under the leeward upper berth and after a day of taking water over the deck, the first time we tacked to port, all the seawater that had accumulated under the starboard upper bunk came cascading down onto the lower starboard bunk completely soaking the foam mattress and rendering that berth unusable for the rest of the voyage.

Rivulets of water would flow down the hull liner next to the navigator's desk. Unused genoa blocks on the gunwale would rattle endlessly like a hammer just inches over the head of one trying to sleep in one of the two dry bunks.

Water was constantly on the cabin sole and by the time we were in the middle of the crossing, we were running low on water in the built-in tanks. I climbed behind the refrigerator into the aft section of the pilot berth to reach the 1/2" vinyl hose. Pulled it out to fill one of the fixed tanks from the 26 gallon flexible water tank. I was surprised to find that the flexible water bag was nearly empty! The screw-on fitting that closed the bag and where I had attached the hose and shut-off valve had completely leaked.

Since our toe rails were leaking so much,

we didn't think that the ever-present wet cabin sole was wet with anything other than seawater. I checked the other 26 gallon flexible tank under the V-berth only to find that, it too, had leaked, leaving only 1/2 a bag of water. This meant we had a little more than 13 gallons to serve 3 guys for the rest of the trip.

I didn't panic. I had purchased reverse osmosis "bags" from a camping supply company. These bags would separate bacteria or salt from water and store the clean water in an outer bag. Of course, this wasn't a high pressure water maker and would take a day to make a pint of potable water. There was also emergency water in the life raft, if things got desperate.

After a week out of St. Pierre, we crossed Flemish Cap, the site of the movie "The Perfect Storm".

We had only 20 knot westerlies and ran on.

Over the seamount of Flemish Cap, we saw our first porpoises, pilot whales and many signs of sea life. I will never forget one evening as the sun set, I was looking aft to see if I would see a "green flash". I had read about green flashes and the theoretical reasons for their occurrence. I had even seen one once, sailing due East past Block Island, RI at dawn. On this occasion, I actually saw two green flashes in rapid succession.

I had planned the dates for this crossing several years in advance. I timed our departure from Newfoundland for a full moon in June, thinking that if we could see icebergs or ships it would be easier with a full moon. As it turned out, we had mostly cloudy skies and couldn't see the moon at all. Luckily, we didn't see any icebergs and were well north of the rhumb line that the commercial shipping from northern Europe to North America used.

The air temperature rose slowly as we left the Labrador current and once we were 200 nm off of Newfoundland, the Raymarine weather graphic device stopped receiving signals from the satellite, but we could still track lows coming from the west with the laptop and the Iridium phone. Around June 15th, we had our first day of sunny skies.

Ben was keen to use the spinnaker and since the west wind had dropped a bit, we raised that sail. The Mate and I took turns trying to keep the spinnaker full and we were able to remove our foul weather gear for the first time in two weeks.

What I failed to realize was that by flying the spinnaker, we raised our downwind speed. That caused the wind generator to stop charging.

SuperWind to the rescue

The next night, while I was sleeping, the Ben and The Mate saw a fishing boat and decided to turn on the radar and the navigation lights. In fact, I think they had every electronic device on board turned on.

The following morning, when I awoke, I saw that the voltage of the batteries was down below 11 volts and the battery selector switch had been left on banks 1 AND 2, so both banks were flat. So flat that we couldn't start the engine. Ben, was sure it was corroded battery terminals, but I had only installed the batteries the year before and had covered the terminals with a corrosion protective spray. Although there were no signs of corrosion, I dutifully cleaned the terminals of all five batteries. The engine still wouldn't start, so we dropped all the sails to allow the wind generator to turn.

After an hour, the voltage rose above 12 volts. I opened all three decompression levers on the Yanmar and Ben hit the start button. The engine turned! I quickly closed the decompression levers and the Yanmar started up. We ran the engine until the batteries were back up to over 13 volts.

I scolded the crew for leaving the battery selector to "All" and running all the electrics without asking the captain. We carried on.

The fair weather continued for a few more days, we continued to run downwind, but without the spinnaker. Only Ben was competent enough to fly the thing. The wind picked up again from the West and The Mate and I made a better course without it.

On the 19th of June, we were approaching the coast of Ireland. We could hear Radio Valencia on the VHF. The skies were still clear, but the wind swung around almost 180° to the southeast and picked up to 20 knots. We began to see fishing boats again and the last of our pilot whales.

On June 22nd, we changed our course to the southeast and began three days of tacking to reach Baltimore, our chosen port of entry. We tacked for three days. Ben wanted to hold a course as close to the wind as possible, but this meant a lot of pounding into the waves and water over the bow.

On my watch, I used the captain's prerogative and cracked off a few degrees to the South, easing the pounding. Our course wasn't as direct to Baltimore, but it was more comfortable and I felt was stressing the ship and crew less.

Ben Morris, God bless him, was a real sail master. He pushed us all the way across the Atlantic, constantly looking to get the most out of *Skylark*.

However, all of the genoa blocks, reefing cheek blocks and the outhaul had seen better days. *Skylark* was 36 years old when she made this crossing. We had replaced all the old systems and rigging, but hadn't started on the cosmetics. I didn't realize that the years of lying in the sun had caused UV damage to the white plastic sheaves. Several sheaves just shattered under the strain of the sheets or the reefing line.

Ben once put some strain on the outhaul and the steel cable that led out of the boom just broke at the welded attachment to the outhaul car. We had old replacement blocks and were able to fix the clew of the mainsail to the end of the boom and were able to keep sailing.

One of the satisfactions of sailing is to be able to jury rig repairs and continue the voyage.

Some of my Irish ancestors had emigrated to the US and had left from Baltimore, Ireland in the 1840s. I thought it was appropriate that I return to that once busy seaport. Baltimore is also an official port of entry to Ireland.

At dawn on June 26th, thirteen days after leaving Cape Race and North America we passed Fastnet Rock on the Southwest corner of Ireland. It was totally foggy and even though we were less than 1nm from the Rock, we couldn't see the lighthouse. We did get a glimpse of a glow in the fog, but that was about it.

We reached Baltimore harbor and dropped the Ben off at his landing near his cottage.

The Mate went ashore to have breakfast with Ben and his parents. I chose to stay aboard, not being familiar with Baltimore harbor and also in the back of my mind, what I was doing by dropping off Ben, allowing him and The Mate to go ashore was illegal. My responsibility as captain dictated that I fly the yellow "Q" flag for quarantine, dock or anchor in Baltimore, go to the pub in the village and ask the barkeeper to contact Irish customs and immigration.

After breakfast, The Mate and I motored over to the town dock in Baltimore. I went to the pub and asked the barkeeper to call immigration and customs. It turned out that a Mr. Maguire wore both hats. I was promised that he would arrive in the afternoon. I asked the barkeeper to ask him if it was alright if I and The Mate could disembark, have a beer and a hot shower while we waited for him. No problem...

By the time we landed at Baltimore on June 26th, 2009, we were down to about a pint of water and had been out of beer for over a week. That first beer in the Baltimore pub tasted fantastic and the shower in the back of the pub was even better!

Mr. Maguire arrived about 2 pm and came to *Skylark* tied up to the town dock. I showed him my ship's papers, zarpe, ship's documentation, radio licenses, &c. When I told him I had departed from Newport, RI., he told me that he knew we had been sailing from Canada. He told me that *Skylark* had been noticed 3 days before by Irish radar and that we were coming from the West. He said he didn't need to check *Skylark* for drug smuggling, as we weren't arriving from the Azores. I suppose the Azores are on the smuggling route from South America.

I mentioned to Mr. Maquire that I was concerned about the time limit of an American boat in the EU.

I asked him when did the 18 month clock started ticking towards the date that I would have to take *Skylark* out of the EU to avoid sales tax and the dreaded Post Construction Assessment survey. When I was in St. Pierre two weeks prior or when we arrived in Ireland?

He said, "Leave your boat in Ireland. We don't care about any of that."

The Mate and I stayed in Baltimore for three days and were lucky to be there when the O'Driscoll family had their annual reunion there.

The O'Driscolls were once kings of southern Ireland and still own or control Cape Clear, a large island near Baltimore, where Gaelic is supposedly in continual use. The nights were full of music and dancing which was quite entertaining for us.

The Mate painted scenes of Baltimore and after a few days, returned to his home in Cincinnati.

I had originally planned to change crew and pickup three Americans in Baltimore, but after a trip alone to Skibberean, a larger town near Baltimore, to replenish the depleted larder and making the trip by public bus, I thought this would be a bit much for the new crew to deal with.

Since I had two days to kill before they arrived, I decided to move the boat alone over to Kinsale, which would be more convenient for the new crew to reach from their airport.

It must be said, that from the time I bought *Skylark,* I really hadn't sailed her that much. Most of my time aboard from 2007 to 2009 was limited to a month or two in the spring or summer and that time was spent on renovations. *Skylark* is also a third bigger than my P26 and much heavier.

The trip to Kinsale from Baltimore appeared

to be a day sail, but as I left Baltimore harbor and headed out into the ocean. I realized that, again, the wind was from the East. The direction I wanted to go. The wind was 20-25 knots, again on the nose. I tacked under the #2 genoa alone and after hours of dealing with sheets that were hung up on mast fixtures, realizing I wasn't going to make Kinsale in daylight, autopilot still not functioning at all, I began to consider my options.

During a previous vacation to this same coastline, my family stayed in a friend's cottage near Schull, I had explored the harbors by car from Mizzen Head to Kinsale.

One particularly picturesque small sheltered harbor came to mind. I looked on the chart plotter and saw that I was directly due South of Glendore.

I sailed towards the mouth of the harbor and carefully minding the buoys, I made my way into the harbor. I dropped the anchor and was almost too tired to make dinner.

Hunger prevailed and I had a nice meal, followed by a movie on the laptop and a good night's rest.

The next morning, I started the engine, raised the anchor and went back to the cockpit to put *Skylark* in gear. Clunk. The engine stopped. I looked around the deck and didn't see any lines that could be in the water. I looked over the stern down into the water and thought I could see a thick line running under the rudder.

Nothing to do but dive down and have a

look. Boy, was that water cold. I knew from my previous land vacations that although the southern coast of Ireland is called the Irish Riviera, the water is cold Atlantic.

Diving under the boat, I could see that there was a very thick mooring line without a mooring buoy, wrapped around the prop shaft and propeller. I went back aboard and not having a bread knife, I took a small saw from the tool box and dove back into the cold water. A few dives and fast sawing enabled me to cut away the line. I reset the anchor and took a hot shower., The engine could heat water for the water heater.

Having recovered from that minor fiasco, I raised the anchor and motored out of Glendore harbor, heading for Kinsale. As I was underway, I passed close to a wooden ketch and saw her name on the transom, *Iolaire*. I remembered that was the name of Don Street's boat that he lived on in the Caribbean. I had read many of Mr. Street's books and one in particular was full of tips for cooking, food selection and even, clothing.

Some of his tips were a bit outdated, especially the bit about leather hip boots, but his tip about wearing unbleached wool socks, I took to heart. I even found them on the internet for $6 a pair. When they arrived, I realized that the socks were US Navy issue. I should have remembered that from my boot camp days. The tip about the socks and wearing a silk aviator's scarf to keep water from running down your neck, I use to this day.

Sunday, June 28th, was a beautiful clear day. The wind was still from the Southeast. Staying close to the coast, I reached Kinsale and negotiated the long channel that runs up to the marina.

I rafted to a yacht that turned out to also just have completed a transAtlantic crossing. The Norwegian owner had purchased a large Valiant double ender and sailed her from New Jersey to Ireland. His Valiant was a real ocean boat and had large tankage for fuel and water. He took the southern route, stopping at the Azores.

Monday, June 29th, my crew, consisting of Rich Doherty, who had helped with the final renovations, Jim Ledogar, a buddy from the boatyard and Carl a friend of his, arrived. Rick and Jim were sailors, but Carl had never sailed at all.

Both of these guys were EMTs working in Manhattan and brought a bag of medical supplies to supplement my already extensive first aid kit.

Otto, the pilot

What they didn't think to bring was seasickness medications. Fortunately, I don't suffer from "mal de mer", but the Mate's sister is a doctor and had loaded us up with several varieties of seasickness medications, including suppositories, the resulting drowsiness of which was offset by dexedrine tablets! This is what jet fighter pilots seem to prefer...

I mention this because as soon as we left Kinsale for Falmouth, England, we were in the ocean no longer than 15 minutes when Carl started chumming. I parked him on the leeward side and when he recovered from his ralphing session, I slapped a Scopalamine patch on his neck and told him to drive the boat.

I explained that keeping one's eye on the horizon alleviated the feeling of seasickness. For the rest of the day, Carl was on the helm. We even fed him his dinner in the cockpit. Later that evening, Carl asked me how was he going to sleep. He was getting tired from being on the helm for 12 hours straight.

I told him that when he could barely keep his eyes open, we would make up his bunk, open his sleeping bag and all he had to do was dive in the sleeping bag and close his eyes. I told him he wouldn't be seasick when he was asleep.

Well, that worked.

The next morning at dawn, Carl came bursting out of the companionway and wanted to take the helm again. He drove the boat all day until we reached Falmouth. We spent a day looking around Falmouth and the famous Pendennis Shipyard where they were putting halyards on a new 50 meter sailboat, that had just finished construction and painting. The turnbuckles on this ship were huge.

The next day found us bound for Cowes on the Isle of Wight. Carl was on the helm for another 18 hour stint at the helm. We began to call him "Otto", short for Ottopilot...

We reached Cowes, got a nice berth at one of the marinas and went off to explore that famous sailor's town. We did some food shopping and I paid a visit to one of the many chandleries there.

As I was browsing in the store, looking for charts of the English Channel and coast of The Netherlands, I happened to see one of the shop's clerks open a drawer. I saw what appeared to be a drawer of white plastic sheaves. Remembering that *Skylark* had several broken cheek blocks and genoa blocks, I asked the clerk if I could bring in my old sheaves for sizing. I ran back to *Skylark* and rounded up all the broken blocks, removing one of the cheek blocks from the reefing system on the boom and returned to the store. I was able to match the OD and width of the sheaves perfectly, but two of them had axle holes that were too small for my blocks' axles. The clerk told me that there was a machinist next door and perhaps he could drill the axle holes to a bit larger diameter. Schaefer advertises that they repair blocks for $99 a piece. I was able to repair four blocks for £16.

Made my day, it did.

The following day, we left Cowes for IJmuiden, the entry to the Amsterdam canal and the route to my destination in Enkhuizen, NL, on the IJsselmeer. We would pass Dover and Rotterdam on the way. The consideration of the heavy shipping to be encountered off of those ports was a bit intimidating.

A day after we left Cowes and Carl aka

"Otto" was on the helm as usual. The guy had helmed *Skylark* all the way from Kinsale, only taking pauses to sleep and make a day's excursion on the Isle of Wight. I asked "Otto" how was he feeling.

He said "Fine."

I asked him when was the last time he changed the Scopalamine patch.

He thought about it for a few seconds and replied, "The day before we reached Cowes."

"Otto," I said. "You are cured from your seasickness. You have been four days with the same patch, the patches are only good for 72 hours and your patch has expired."

We passed Brighton and thought about stopping, but I was nearing 3 months of being away from home and had left my wife alone with our two small boys. She hadn't been happy when I left, she was even more unhappy after the SPOT device saga and the thought of having to reimburse the Canadian Coast Guard $125,000. I was in a little bit of a hurry to get home and face the music.

Passing Dover was exciting since it was a major ferry haven and high speed hydrofoils and large ferry boats were passing back and forth from England to the continent.

Passing close to Maasmund (Maas is the name of the river that flows past Antwerp and Rotterdam and mund = mouth) there are specific instructions on the paper charts that recreational vessels must pass Massmund close inshore at 90°

through a special traffic lane for recreational yachts and radio Maasmund Control of one's intentions.

Maasmund Control will give the yacht permission to pass if there are no ships leaving or entering the river.

As it was dark when we passed, it was disconcerting to see so many ships at anchor or moving slowly in the English Channel.

What was even worse was that the ships leaving Maasmund about every two minutes had their running lights hardly visible against all the lights on shore. Looking carefully and closely, one could only see a black shape blocking the shore lights.

People often ask me what was the hairiest part of *Skylark's* Atlantic crossing and I always say it was the northern end of the English Channel. By now, the 30 knot wind had turned to the Northwest and the seas were up to 2 meters. It was exhilarating night sailing to say the least.

Around 4 am, we were approaching the entrance to the Amsterdam canal at IJmuiden. I looked at the chart-plotter to get an idea of what the entrance to the canal looked like.

At IJmuiden, there are two long stone jetties that lead West from the shore. It appeared that there would be enough room to drop the mainsail in between the two jetties, as long as there wasn't a lot of shipping traffic coming out of the Amsterdam canal into the Channel.

When I told the crew that we were nearing IJmuiden and would have to lower the sails to enter the marina, they wanted to do that out in the North Sea. With the 30 knot wind, the dark night and the two meter waves, I decided to drop the sails inside and in the flatter water between the jetties. The crew didn't like that idea and it was the first time in the whole voyage from North America where I overruled the crew's opinion. Fortunately, I was proven correct and there was plenty of room inside the jetties and there were no ships leaving Amsterdam canal at 0400.

We entered the large marina at IJmuiden and motored around the docks until we found a suitable empty berth, which unfortunately, turned out to be the farthest berth from the harbor offices. I needed to report *Skylark's* continental arrival and would have to call Dutch immigration and customs. Since it was 0400, I thought we all could catch a little sleep and wait until the marina offices opened.

Around 1100, two officers from the Dutch immigration and customs showed up on the dock and wanted to board. One was older and quite large, the other was younger and thin, they reminded me of Laurel and Hardy.

I presented *Skylark's* papers and the crew's passports. All of us were US citizens, I had a resident's visa for Germany, Rick had his return air ticket, but Jim and Carl, the two EMTs only had e-Tickets. The older Dutch officer obviously had no idea what an e-Ticket was. Simply a piece of paper with some text and a barcode, which when scanned by a machine at the airport, would produce a boarding pass.

He asked them what they did for work and they replied that they were emergency medical technicians working in Manhattan. He still didn't quite understand, but when they mentioned "call 911", he thought that they were referring to September 11th and his demeanor softened.

Then the big guy got up and squeezed his large girth into the V-berth. He started moving piles of baggage and cans of paint around in the V-berth, I couldn't imagine what he thought he was looking for. Pygmies? There wasn't room in the V-berth for anything unless I was smuggling pygmies from Africa and had a couple buried under the pile of teak.

The Locks

Anyway, we were cleared and allowed to pass into The Netherlands. We still had a nine hour trip from IJmuiden to Enkhuizen on the IJsselmeer ahead of us.

My German sailing friend, Captain Mike had told me that he would meet *Skylark* at the marina in IJmuiden and guide us on to Enkhuizen. When Mike showed up, we got under way, left the marina and *Skylark* met her first lock.

Those of us who sail the coastline of the US, don't usually meet locks. Swing bridges, drawbridges are about the only impediments to our sailing that we deal with. Northern Europe is full of locks and in the five years of *Skylark's* residence in Europe, she has met dozens of locks. *Skylark* was still "new" to me and although I had sailed her quite a bit by now, I didn't have a lot of experience maneuvering her in close quarters.

I certainly had no experience in dealing with locks. The Dutch use locks to move vessels between bodies of water that have different levels. Sometimes the difference between the level of the North Sea and the level of the water in the IJsselmeer is the same, sometimes there is a 2 meter difference.

There are many considerations to make when entering a lock. First, one has to know the signals from the lockkeeper, red and green lights and combinations that mean "enter", "do not enter", "soon enter". Then, what other type of vessels you are entering the lock with, the direction of the wind and other influences have to be considered before finding your place in the lock.

This is not the place to go into all the harrowing experiences I had in the following five years of negotiating locks in Holland and Scotland. Needless to say, *Skylark* had a flawless Awlgrip® paint job in 2007 and she is in need of a new topside paint job in 2014.

Passing two locks, one at IJmuiden, one at Amsterdam, crossing the Markermeer to a lock that emptied us into the IJsselmeer found us in

Enkhuizen. Captain Mike, who keeps his boat in Compagnieshaven, the marina I had reserved a slip in, led *Skylark* to her new home in Holland.

The crew was starving and not interested in cooking on board, so we walked into the quaint 16th century village of Enkhuizen. It was well after 2100 and the restaurants were closed or no longer serving. We found Georgio's, a late night pizza joint that also served decent ribs and steaks.

The following morning my wife arrived with my two small sons. The boys were glad to see me and wanted to see *Skylark*. The wife was still mad at me for leaving her with the boys for so long and was still waiting for the $125,000 Canadian bill from the Canadian coast guard for the SAR mission off the coast.

She was still mad at me two years later...

Importing Skylark

Since *Skylark* arrived in 2009, she has sailed to The Channel Islands, France, the Isle of Wight, Scotland for The Whisky Tour, Helgoland, an island in the North Sea and had a 23 hour tow from Tiel, NL, up the Rhine river by riverboat to Cologne, Germany where she wintered over and got new toe-rails, coaming caps and interior hull liner of Miranti lathing.

When I first moved to the EU, the law stated that I had to take the boat out of the EU every six months or else pay VAT and have a Post Construction Assessment survey to have the whole boat "CE" marked.

Easy, I thought. Just sail *Skylark* to The Channel Islands every so often to reset the clock.

Then Brussels changed the law from six months to 18 months, still easy.

Then the rules changed again. If one was a "resident" of the EU, one had to pay VAT and have a PCA within one month after arriving in the EU.

So in 2011, I paid the VAT on *Skylark's* purchase price, not her value. I went through a customs broker and I was surprised that no one wanted to even look at *Skylark* for valuation. Cool.

When I received the documentation of the VAT being paid, I complained to the customs broker that the VAT form was printed with an old fashioned dot matrix printer. There was no agency or government logo anywhere. The whole thing looked like a bad homemade forgery. The broker assured me that all over Europe, the authorities would only be interested in the VAT number and could check that number and the validity of *Skylark* tax status.

In 2013, I was torn between having *Skylark's* topsides repainted or paying for a PCA. The prices were about the same. €3000.

Since I was planning to do some harbor-hopping in France in the summer of 2014, I would be better off having a scratched boat with all my licenses, USCG documentation, VAT receipt and PCA number with CE mark than a shiny new boat with no PCA, subjecting me to a €5000 fine.

I have read that the French are notorious for fine combing a foreign-flagged vessel for expired flares (€75 PER each out-dated flare) and incorrect paperwork. The Norwegians and Swedes are famous for asking for VAT and PCA documents.

Together, paying the VAT and the PCA added a bit more than $7000 to what I paid for *Skylark*.

Including all the new appliances, equipment, labor costs to various helpers and paperwork in the US and the EU, I have a bit more than $80,000 invested. What I got for my money is a boat that is worth more than $150,000 and has all new systems.

Not to mention that I am now personally acquainted with every screw, nut and bolt in the boat.

I have a preference for preventive maintenance and maintaining a new system removes the uncertainty of maintaining equipment of an undertermined history.

Prior to partaking in the www.worldcruising.com's 2012 Whisky Tour, I stripped the old gelcoat and bottom paint from *Skylark* and added a new Gelshield bottom and many layers of International Micron. *Skylark's* previous bottom painting lasted four years in salt and fresh water.

There were only three barnacles on the whole bottom. Sailing from fresh water in the IJsselmeer to salt water in the North Sea and back, seems to kill any barnacles and algae that want to grow on the bottom.

In anticipation of anchoring in kelp and amongst rocks, I considered buying a Luke storm anchor that would disassemble into three pieces for stowage. I installed a Flexofold 15" two-bladed propeller and a flexible coupling. I didn't want to go diving under the boat in cold Scottish waters to cut a crab trap line off of the propeller. I also bought an extendable tree limb saw, so that if *Skylark* did pick up a line, I could possibly cut it away without swimming..

Personal Gear

A good crew knows what to pack:

• Soft vinyl waterproof duffel bag with no wheels. Wheels leave marks on hull liners and cabin soles. Ortlieb or Northface make good dry sacks.

• Personal life jacket or vest, one that is inflatable and has a crotch strap and harness built-in. A personal strobe light, small personal EPIRB, a loud whistle are good things to attach to the life vest. Check with your airline about flying with a gas cartridge for your life jacket.

• Sleeping bag with cotton insert I recommend a full-size sleeping bag, not a mummy sack. Coleman makes different models of sleeping bags that can keep one warm down to -30F. A flat cotton bed sheet sewn on three sides, leaving one end open can be used for an insert for more comfort and it is easier to remove the cotton insert and wash it, than to wash the complete sleeping bag.

• Pillow (feather pillows can be compacted more than a Hollofill pillow)

• Unbleached wool socks (US Navy issue socks can be found online from army surplus suppliers for around $6 a pair)

• Silk long underwear and undershirt, one can also use merino or alpaca wool which is quite soft and doesn't itch) silk and wool are warm when wet

- Heavy weight wool sweater (US Navy issue mock turtleneck sweaters are great, but any thick wool sweater will suffice)

- Heavy weight wool pants (German army battle trousers with dacron from the front of the upper thigh to below the knee are less than $40 and suitable for cold weather when there isn't too much water on deck)

- Silk scarf for neck (white aviator's scarves can be found on the internet for around $25)

- Wool watch cap or warm hat of your choice (US Navy watch caps itch but they don't blow off in a strong wind and there are merino or cashmere watch caps available

- Foul weather jacket (this is no place to pinch pennies). Henri Lloyd, Musto make top of the line gear with features that make the investment worthwhile. Foul weather pants (see above - consider a pair with a unzippable fly. Having to remove all your gear just to have a pee is a real nuisance)

- Sea boots (DuBarry or Musto make Gortex and leather boots that while they are pricey, they are more comfortable than all rubber boots. I do wear white shrimper's boots, which are white because they are cooler to wear in the hot sun on a hot deck. They also don't leave black marks on the boat's deck. They are also called butcher's boots.

- Deck shoes for when the weather is warm and dry. Not to be worn on land, street shoes not to be worn aboard

- Several cotton underpants, several cotton undershirts

- Large rubber gloves with wool gloves as liners. (wool dries quickly and is warm when wet) This is the best system to keep your hands dry and warm. I haven't found any really waterproof sailing gloves

- Two pairs of eyeglasses if needed for distance or chart reading

- Two pairs of sunglasses

- Some kind of retainer attachment method for glasses

- Seasickness meds of your choice, even if you don't think you get seasick, one should have some along anyway. Scopalomine patches are best for most sailors, but one who is susceptible to seasickness should experiment with different compounds or other techniques to avoid this annoying problem.

- Headlamp for night reading

- A personal hand-held GPS

- Folding knife with locking blade, best is an automatic knife with a serrated blade for cutting lines.

- Personal music player with headphones

- Eyeshades and earplugs

- Keeping all your kit IN your bag at all times and not leaving dirty socks lying around the cabin makes one a desirable crewmate. Often, I tell the crew that stray or roaming personal items will be confiscated and auctioned to the highest bidder at the end of the cruise. Proceeds going to the fuel kitty.

- Personal hygiene: package of butt wipes for washing feet, etc. Soap and shampoo, not all marinas supply these items for their guests, personal hygiene is important for the comfort of all.

Note: for older sailors suffering from prostate issues, various seasickness meds can severely aggravate the problem, completely preventing one from peeing. I have added two Foley catheters to my medicine kit and if one isn't sure that a catheter will be available, one can bring some of one's own.

If you carry an umbrella, it usually won't rain.

Notes:

Skylark's Survey

Skylark's 2007 Survey prior to purchasing

Note: I contacted Boat/US who held my insurance policy on both my boats and asked them for their recommendation of surveyor in or near Connecticut where *Skylark* was berthed. I contracted Mr. Bill Coble to drive to the marina where *Skylark* was on the hard.

He emailed me the evening after he made the survey of *Skylark* and told me that there were so many problems, I probably wouldn't be interested in her and I could save some money if he didn't have to write up the survey report. I asked him to go ahead with the report and list the worst problems first.

WILLIAM COBLE
Independent Marine Surveyor
P.O. Box 1434
North Kingstown, Rhode Island 02852
tel/fax 401 295 1389 cobleboatsurveys@cox.net

12 June 2007

Mr. George DuBose
Hof 242/Wonderland
Bonnerstr. 242
50968 Cologne, Germany

Re: *"SKYLARK"* 1973 Pearson 36' fiberglass sloop
H.I.N. PEA510580473
Federal documentation number 558537 net 17
Hailing port is Philadelphia PA
Built by Pearson Yachts, Portsmouth,
Rhode Island
Hull number 58

Dear Mr. DuBose,
At your request I inspected the above boat on 6 June 2007 at Bruce and Johnson Boatyard in Branford, Connecticut. The boat was inspected while stored ashore.

This purchase survey was done for the exclusive use of the client listed above. It is not transferable to any other person or entity. The intended users of the report are the client and those underwriters insuring this boat for this owner only. This letter is my written report describing my observations and recommendations.

Scope of Survey:
The survey of this boat is based solely on a careful visual and non-destructive inspection of all accessible portions of its structure and available equipment. Complete inspection can be made only by the removal of laminates, flats, soles, headliners, hull liners, tanks, joinerwork and coatings. This would be destructive in nature and prohibitively time consuming, therefore was not done.

Complete inspection of machinery, piping, systems, tanks, electronics, electrical equipment and electrical wiring can only be made by continuous operation or by disassembly. This has not been done.

As the mast was stepped, inspection of the mast and rig was limited to that which could be observed from deck level.

Work items marked with an asterisk * are those I feel should be corrected/accomplished to meet underwriter's requirements.

General:

This boat is a fiberglass sloop. Propulsion is by a diesel engine. The boat has a moderate fin keel and a rudder that is fully supported by a skeg. Digital photos were taken during the inspection. If your insurance company would like copies of the photos they can email me at the address above and I will send the photos within 48 hours.

Hull and Structural:

The hull is a solid fiberglass laminate. The hull is stiffened by a structural fiberglass hull liner, by fiberglass transverse floors and by bulkheads and joinerwork fiberglass tabbed to the hull interior. Fiberglass tabbing was inspected throughout the boat. There were no significant tabbing failures. Note the slight tabbing failures at the aft end of the starboard settee and in the starboard forward hanging locker. Note that the builder neglected to install tabbing aft at the port settee. * Install tabbing at this location. This should probably be done when the boat is in its natural shape afloat.

The hull-to-deck connection is made with an inside flange. Mechanical fasteners are stainless steel bolts. No deficiencies were observed. Note the fiberglass repair port forward at the hull to deck connection.

Note the minor deflections of the hull at the aft boat stand pads and at the port middle stand. The hull should regain most of its original shape after the boat is launched. In the future suggest locating the boat stand pads more in line with interior structural members.

Moisture meter readings (Protimeter Surveymaster Meter) taken on the topsides were 13 units and lower. These are low readings.

Moisture meter readings taken on underwater portions of the hull were 11 units and lower. These are low readings. Readings taken on the lower portion of the skeg were to 22 units (moderately high). There were no other negative indications at the skeg.

Moisture meter readings taken on the rudder were 16 units and lower. These are low readings for a rudder.

There were no indications of osmotic blistering on underwater portions of the hull.

Underwater portions of the hull were sounded with a plastic hammer. There were no indications of delamination.

The outside ballast keel is lead. Stainless steel keel bolts are installed in double rows. The seam between the keel and the hull is not visible. This indicates good holding by the keel bolts. There were no indications of grounding damage to the keel or the keel supporting structure.

The white epoxy putty installed forward of the mast step was probably installed to prevent water from sitting in this location.

A hull drain plug fitting is installed low in the bilge sump. Removing the plug when the boat is stored ashore will prevent possible accumulation of water in the bilge during out of the water storage.

The mast of this boat steps on the keel structure. The steel mast step has been coated with a rust treatment. No deficiencies were observed.

The headstay chainplate is fastened to the stem. The shroud chainplates are fastened to bulkheads and fiberglass webs. The backstay chainplate is fastened to the transom. Note the fiberglass repair at the top of the port forward lower chainplate web.

There has been leaking at the shroud chainplates. There is water damage to the ash plywood hull liners at the aft lower shroud chainplates. Very high moisture meter readings taken at the hull liners indicate there is still leaking. Because of the leaking at the chainplates there is the possibility of crevice corrosion to the stainless steel where it passes through the deck (where no one can see). The chainplates should be removed for a full inspection. * Do this.

2.0 Deck, Deckhouse, Cockpit and Deck Fittings:

The deck is a fiberglass laminate with an end-grain balsa core added to provide stiffening. Walking portions have molded non-skid. Traction is good.

Moisture meter readings taken on the deck were generally 11 units and lower. These are low readings. The only elevated reading I was able to take was to 22 units (moderately high) at the starboard side deck cowl.

The deck is mostly covered with Treadmaster that is epoxied to the deck. I understand the Treadmaster was installed ten years ago. At a few areas the edges are beginning to peel.

Note that because of the installation of the Treadmaster I could not use my moisture meter on most of the deck. I would anticipate that any boat this age has some level of moisture intrusion in the deck core.

Deck fittings are installed using bedding compound that acts like a gasket to prevent leaking. Suggest re-bedding any deck fittings that show symptoms of leaking. This will prevent deck leaks and will prevent possible damage to the deck core.

Single vinyl covered lifelines supported by stainless steel stanchions run from the bow pulpit aft to the stern rail. The lifeline covers are cracking. Gates are provided port and starboard. The lifeline stanchions are secured in their bases by machine screws. All were secure. The stanchion bases were secure except for number 3 port base that is loose enough to allow leaking. Suggest tightening the through bolts at this stanchion base.

Note the flexing of the deck when force is applied to the lifeline stanchions.

Note the play at the pulpit bases.

Note the bent forward brace at the port gate.

A stainless steel fold-down boarding ladder is installed at the transom. With the ladder in the up position it may be difficult to board the boat from the water without assistance. Suggest installing an emergency boarding ladder at a rail. This device would allow a person in the water to pull on a lanyard to deploy the ladder.

Hasps are installed at the port and starboard cockpit locker lids. Lanyards are installed for securing the lids in the open position.

The lazarette hatch is secured in the closed position by a line that runs to the port cockpit locker. A bungee cord is installed for securing the hatch in the open position.

The exterior teak is very worn with some cracking and many missing bungs. It generally needs replacement rather than refinishing.

One short teak grabrail is installed port forward on the deckhouse top. Note that the grabrail has thinned after years of weathering. You should install grabrails port and starboard on the deckhouse top.

The dodger is supported by an aluminum frame. The dodger was not aboard.

A new starboard bow chock was partially installed. It does not match the port bow chock. You should fix the 1" hole in the cockpit port wall. Note the deteriorating plywood backing plates at the undersides of the cockpit combings.

Paints and Coatings:

The topside finish is a dark blue Imron finish that I understand was applied in 2002. There is a gold molded cove stripe and a white boot top stripe. Appearance is very good from a distance. Note that the dark color allows one to see fiberglass print-through (the pattern of the fiberglass cloth) everywhere, several hard spots at bulkheads and a few areas of underlying gelcoat crazing. There are only a few minor scratches to the finish itself.

The deck and deckhouse finish is white gelcoat and paint. Note the painting not done at the starboard side deck between the Treadmaster panels. Appearance of the deck is fair to good. There is minor deck gelcoat crazing.

The new red bottom paint is in very good condition except for moderate underlying flaking.

Interior:

The interior is fully finished and provides accommodations for cruising. The headliner is a fiberglass molding. A fiberglass hull liner forms the sole and some of the furniture bases. Bulkheads and cabinets are built of solid teak, teak plywood and wood-grain Formica covered plywood. The cabin was clean. Appearance is good given the boat's age.

Note the deterioration of the non-structural plywood panel outboard of the starboard settee. Note the deterioration of the woodwork port aft in the cabin.

It was wet under the port settee cushion.

* Fix the loose hinge fasteners at the companionway steps.

The forward emergency escape hatch functioned fully. The gasket needs to be replaced. The hatch is heavily crazed. Suggest replacing the glazing.

There were no indications of leaking at the fixed ports.

Suggest installing non-skid strips on the companionway steps.

The interior cushions old but usable.

The cabin doors worked fully except for the

latch at the head door.

U.S.C.G. required plastics disposal warning notice is posted.

5.0 Spars and Rigging:

This is a masthead rig with one set of aluminum spreaders. There is a roller furling headstay, upper shrouds, double lower shrouds and a fixed backstay. * Install cotter pins at the backstay turnbuckle.

The mast, boom and whisker pole are aluminum extrusions. No deficiencies were observed.

Suggest unstepping the mast next winter in order to allow a full inspection of the mast heel and mast step. The mast heel has been coated with an anti-corrosion product.

Note that the port upper shroud chainplate turnbuckle is a replacement that does match the other turnbuckles.

The winches worked.
The sails were not aboard.
The mainsail cover was not aboard.
Suggest replacing the aging mastboot.
The gooseneck fitting is in good condition.
The running rigging has minor to moderate wear. It all appears serviceable.

The stainless steel wire rope standing rigging appears to be in good condition. The lower end fittings appear to be in good condition.

Propulsion, Control and Steering:
Propulsion is by a replacement Yanmar four cylinder fresh water cooled diesel engine. The engine is clean. The paint is in very good condition. There is no rust. The engine is supported by four flexible mounts on fiberglass beds. No deficiencies were observed.

The engine was not operated or evaluated as part of the inspection.

I understand that the engine was installed in 2005 and has had very little use.

There is no engine hour meter.

Engine is model 3GM30F/serial number is 22899. I understand that the cable kill switch is new. Coolant level was correct at the coolant bottle. The two vee belts are in very good condition.

U.S.C.G. required oil discharge warning notice is posted.

The cockpit engine panel provides a tachometer and warning lights and an alarm system. The ignition is secured by a key. The three warning lights tested okay. Note the coolant light lamp test switch. The low oil pressure alarm worked.

Two lever cable throttle and shift controls are installed. The controls worked. The levers are color-coded and labeled.

The exhaust system was replaced along with the engine. The engine wet exhaust discharges through a fiberglass muffler and exhaust hoses. The hoses are in very good condition. The exhaust hose connections are secured by doubled hose clamps. The cooling water injection hose is fitted with a vented loop.

Note that extended cranking of a non-starting marine engine can fill the exhaust system with seawater that can back into the combustion chambers. After 30 seconds of cranking the engine intake seacock should be closed until the engine starts. Remember to open the seacock when the engine starts.

The engine and transmission turn a stainless steel shaft and a bronze two blade right hand propeller. The propeller is in very good condition. The shaft is supported by a single leg bronze strut. There was no play in the cutless bearing. The shaft is not in contact with the shaft log.

I understand that the shaft, propeller, cutless bearing and shaft seal were replaced when the new engine was installed.

The shaft seal is dripless cooling water injection type. The bellows jumper hose is in very good condition. The hose ends are secured by doubled hose clamps.

Steering is by wheel via chain and cable to or plumbed. The toilet currently discharges to a a bronze quadrant on the bronze rudderstock. The steering worked. The rudderstock packing gland is bronze.

The wheel brake worked.

The rudder stops worked.

Where they are inspectable the steering cables are in good condition.

The steering cables are properly tensioned.

There was no play in the lower rudder bearing.

7.0 Piping, Tanks and Systems:

The underwater through hull fittings are bronze seacocks. The only seacock that worked was the engine intake seacock that appears to be a replacement. * Free up the other seacocks.

The hoses attached to the seacocks are in good condition. Some of the seacock hose connections are secured by single hose clamps. It is conventional to install doubled hose clamps. Suggest installing second hose clamps if the seacock barbs are long enough to accept second hose clamps.

Suggest closing the seacocks when leaving the boat unattended. The cockpit scupper seacocks must be left open.

The engine intake has an interior seawater strainer.

Monel fuel tank is installed under the cockpit. The tank is secured by gasketed galvanized steel straps.

The fuel fill hose is in good condition.

The fuel fill hose ends are secured by doubled hose clamps.

The deck fuel fill fitting is labeled "GAS"* Eliminate this label and provide a "DIESEL" label.

The fuel hoses and lines are rated.

A Racor fuel filter/water separator is installed. The fuel line shut-off valve at the Racor worked.

The fuel tank vent discharge fitting is installed to port at the transom. Suggest installing mesh in the discharge fitting (to keep bugs out).

Fiberglass fresh water tanks are installed under the port and starboard settees. The tanks are secured by fiberglass tabbing. The tanks fill at the tank tops. Pressure hot and cold water is supplied to the galley and head sinks.

The fresh water tank gate valves worked. There was no water in the tanks so I could not fully test the fresh water system. The pressure pump ran. The fresh water in-line strainer plastic housing is broken.

The hand pump at the galley sink is probably the icebox drain.

The 110 volt water heater/heat exchanger is installed forward in the starboard cockpit locker. The water heater is secure. The pressure relief valve was free.

A new plastic waste holding tank is in position under the vee berth. The tank is not secured

Lectra san MSD that is not compliant with waste regulations. Suggest plumbing the waste system so the toilet discharges to the holding tank without direct overboard discharge. This would allow you to eliminate the two vented loops.

The manual toilet pump could not be tested with the boat out of the water.

A 12 volt submersible bilge pump and a float switch are installed in the bilge. The pump worked automatically.

Suggest installing a high bilge water alarm. This would consist of a float switch wired to an alarm.

A manual diaphragm bilge pump is installed at the helm. A pick-up strainer is installed in the bilge. The pump developed suction when I operated it.

There is no cookstove. The remote pressure alcohol tank from the original cookstove is still installed.

A Force 10 LPG vented cabin heater is installed. Operating instructions are posted. Clearances are adequate. The LPG cylinder installs on deck aft. Note that the boat does not come with an LPG cylinder.

When the boat is closed up the cabin is ventilated by two forward facing cowls installed at the side decks and cowls/dorades installed port and starboard of the mast partners.

A cowl is installed over the rode locker. The solar vent installed in the lazarette hatch worked.

The engine compartment is ventilated naturally by two aft facing cowls installed at the stern rail. The ventilation hoses are in good condition except for a tear in the port hose. The compartment is ventilated mechanically by a 12 volt discharge blower. The blower worked.

The vent hole at the forward engine compartment panel must be intended to provide air to the engine compartment. It will also increase engine noise in the cabin.

Suggest installing a battery-powered or 12 volt smoke detector/CO monitor.

A bonding system is installed.

Ground wires installed at the chainplates indicate the boat has a lightning protection system.

8.0 Electrical, Electronics and Navigation:

Two 12 volt batteries are installed in the starboard cockpit locker. The forward battery is in a plastic battery case bottom. * Provide a case bottom for the aft battery. * Secure the batteries. * Install battery case lids or positive terminal caps.

The 12 VDC electrical distribution panel provides 10 labeled fuse protected 12 volt circuits. Suggest labeling the switch on/off positions.

A 4-position battery switch is installed. Do not turn the switch to the off position when the engine is running.

The interior lights are protected. All worked except the one port aft at the vee berth. There is no bulb at the articulating light at the nav table.

I could not see if an anchor light is installed. If there is no anchor light at the masthead you can hang a portable anchor light on the headstay.

The bow and stern navigation lights worked. I could not see if the steaming light worked. * Check this light at night.

The spreader and foredeck lights did not work.

The three cabin fans worked. Note the exposed wiring connections at the port forward fan.

The 110 volt system was not operated.

The 110 volt circuits are fuse protected.

A weatherproof 110 volt inlet fitting is installed.

Note the scorched wire at the back of the 110 volt inlet fitting. * Fix this before operating the system.

110 volt wiring is stranded type.

Suggest adding GFCI protection to the 110 volt outlet circuit.

A microwave oven was aboard.

A Newmar RM 15 amp automatic battery charger is installed. It plugs into the outlet circuit.

A 2005 Carrier recreational vehicle 110 volt air-conditioner has been installed in the salon hatch space.

A Sanyo 110 volt refrigerator/freezer is installed in the cookstove space. * Secure the refrigerator.

Electronics are:

Apelco LDR 3900 radar.

Standard VHF radio.

Sailing instruments: apparent wind/boat speed and log/windspeed/depth.

Dual AM/FM/CD stereo, worked.

The seller declined to demonstrate the operation of the electronics.

Note that the wiring connections for the sailing instruments are twisted wire and tape.

An E.S. Ritchie compass is installed at the helm. Suggest checking the compass against a known heading.

* Provide other U.S.C.G. required safety equipment: a first aid kit, a horn and three current flares.

Suggest wearing inflatable lifejackets.

Ground tackle: A small Danforth anchor (too small for the boat) is ready to use in hangers on the bow pulpit. A chain and good rode are attached. Note the rust on the chain. Suggest seizing the shackles. The spare anchor is a folding anchor with attached chain and fair rode.

A.B.Y.C. requires three mounted portable fire extinguishers on a boat this length and the cabin extinguishers must have type ABC capacity. Three expired fire extinguishers were aboard.*

Mount ABC extinguishers forward and aft in the cabin and mount a BC extinguisher at the helm (inside a cockpit locker).

Conclusions:

Provided the items marked with an asterisk are corrected/accomplished, I feel the boat would be a suitable insurance risk for bays, sounds and coastal waters provided a qualified crew is aboard, and giving due regard to weather and sea conditions. er and sea conditions.

Based on its general good condition and its level of equipment, and giving consideration to the replacement diesel engine, I feel the current fair market value of this boat is $40,000. Replacement value (same boat, brand new) is approximately $160,000.

The European Union
Post Construction Assessment Survey

I suppose that originally, the idea of a Post Construction Assessment survey was formulated to syncronise the construction methods and materials across the European Union for safety and environmental issues. Not only were these regulations to be implemented by European boat manufacturers, but for any manufacturer who wished to place their new boats into the EU market.

Similar to the safety stipulations specified in the standards of the American Boat and Yacht Council, the Underwriters Laboratory and the US Coast Guard, unfortunately the standards between the Recreational Craft Directive and the US standards organizations are not the same. Yacht racing organizations have additional and even more stringent regulations.

When we started *Skylark's* renovations, I was only focussing on the standards of the ABYC and the USCG. For most of *Skylark's* new equipment, this was a non-issue. All of her Raymarine electronics are CE marked. Her engine, although not marked with a CE, I was able to obtain from my US Yanmar parts dealer, a CE certificate for a 2005 Yanmar 3GM30F in Dutch. *Skylark's* water heater, toilet, refrigerator, the ProTech1240iPLUS 40 Amp battery charger, the Eno Gasgone oven and stereo all have CE marks.

What wasn't marked with a CE was my propane system. I had purchased Worthington gas

Non Conformity surveying department			DCI

Form no.	1	Project no.	1300.13
Client	George DuBose	Product	Sailing vessel sloop
Reference	PCA	Project manager	RB
Status			

NC no.	Date	Guideline & Standards	Non compliance	Accepted on / by
1	4-11-2013	ISO 15085	The intermediate line in the guard rail is missing	
2	Dito	ISO 10240	Owners manual is not on board	
3	Dito	ISO 12216	Window Port side after is leaking	
4	Dito	ISO 10088	Fuel filter is executed with glass or plastic bottom	
5	Dito	ISO 15083 En 8099	In Bilge pump system on/off switch is missing	

This is the very short list of Skylark's "defects" determined by the Dutch inspector. I was very suprised when he told me that after I made these modifications and some others that are not madatory, he would certify Skylark with an RCD "A" catagory. I was hoping for at least a "B" designation. Between the Jordan Series drogue, removing the cockpit speakers, the well-tied down batteries, the extra 1/4" aluminum plate that fits behind the companionway boards, I think Skylark could survive a direct hit by a 10 meter breaking wave or a rollover.

bottles that were made from thick-walled aluminum and rust proof, a Trident two bottle fiberglass locker, Trident rubber gas hose and Trident gas alarm system. None of these items were CE marked and not only unmarked, the European regulations state that the gas line be made of flexible copper tubing. What really put me off was that according to the EU regs, the copper tubing could not pass directly through a bulkhead.

A fitting had to be installed in the bulkhead and one tube was fitted to one side of the bulkhead and then the gas line was continued by being fitted to the other side of the fitting!

In my mind, this meant two possible gas leaks at every bulkhead pass-through. I thought that the ABYC standards were superior. They specify that each appliance be fed by it's own gas line that started at the gas regulator inside the gas locker and ended at the appliance. No fittings anywhere along the rubber hose. The hose itself is fire resistant and purpose built for propane.

My Force 10 Cozy Cabin propane heater was probably as old as the boat and when the thermocoupling failed, I found that Force 10 had sold its manufacturing rights for the Cozy Cabin heater to Sig Marine, a Canadian firm. The Sig Marine unit was basically the same, but the gas controls, thermocoupling and piezo lighter had been modernized. When I had to buy the complete new assembly for the gas and flame regulator, I got a new manual covering the appliance. No CE mark was mentioned in the manual or marked on the new burner assembly.

This was my biggest worry about putting *Skylark* through the PCA. I was afraid that the inspector would condemn my new gas system and I would have to replace the rubber hose with copper line and maybe the gas bottles and all the accessories.

I was thinking I would just pull the whole propane system out, get the CE mark for *Skylark* and then reinstall the system. I wasn't going to install copper gas lines.

Fortunately the Dutch inspector was a clever gentleman and could understand that this ABYC-coded installation was safe and practical.

When I started reading about the difference in the CE safety regulation vs. ABYC/USCG, I read that it was possible to submit documents and apply for a CE mark by one's self, Ha! Contacting the Royal Yacht Association, joining the RYA to gain access to free legal advice, produced no information about self-documentation.

I started contacting naval architects in the UK and Holland and enquiring about the cost of these "inspections". I found a company in Enkhuizen, *Skylark's* European home and was quoted a price of over 4000 euros, I contacted an English company and was quoted over 3000 euros, and I don't know if that would have covered the inspector's travel costs.

Still searching for information about how one could do this on one's own, I emailed DCI, a Dutch firm in Joure, NL and asked how I could file this PCA documentation by myself.

Again, all I got was a price quote for the PCA survey. Well, at least this time the price was down to 2700 euros plus 21% VAT!

I was leery of giving the inspection firm the exact location of *Skylark,* since according to the

EU law, I should have had *Skylark* inspected BEFORE sailing her in Europe. By law, one is supposed to pay the VAT in the first European land upon which the vessel lands.

There have been numerous magazine articles in the European yachting press about horror stories of obaining a CE mark for a vessel built outside of the EU. I read that a man had bought a boat in Vancouver, Canada, sailed her south along the North American west coast to the Panamanian Canal, then across the Atlantic to the UK and when he put his vessel through the PCA inspection, he was only granted the RCD "D" catagory. The guy just sailed halfway around the world and some bureaucrat says his boat isn't safe to go offshore. I read that the "righting" moment and other specifications had to be calculated by naval architecture formulas or by actual testing of the boat, which can lead to damage or destruction of the vessel.

What happens if a boat is not CE marked?

Non compliance is a criminal offence and is enforced by Trading Standards Officers with penalties of up to £5,000 &/or 3 months imprisonment. Operators can encounter difficulties when travelling from state to state or when selling their craft within the European market without appropriate documentation.

There is a real risk that should a non-com

pliant craft be involved in a marine accident it will be traced back to the builder or importer who could be considered to be negligent.

Design Categories

A. **Ocean**: Designed for extended voyages where conditions may exceed wind force 8 (Beaufort scale) and significant wave heights of 4 m and above but excluding abnormal conditions, and vessels largely self-sufficient.

B. **Offshore:** Designed for waves of up to 4m significant height and a wind of Beaufort force 8 or less. Such conditions may be encountered on offshore voyages of sufficient length or on coasts where shelter may not always be immediately available. Such conditions may also be experienced on inland seas of sufficient size for the wave height to be generated.

C. **Inshore:** Designed for waves of up to 2m significant height and a typical steady wind force of Beaufort force 6 or less. Such conditions may be encountered on exposed inland waters, and in coastal waters in moderate weather conditions.

D. **Sheltered Waters:** Designed for voyages on sheltered coastal waters, small bays, small lakes, rivers and canals when conditions up to, and including, wind force 4 and significant wave heights up to, and including, 0.3m may be experienced, with occasional waves of 0.5m maximum height, for example from passing vessels.

Meeting the CE inspector

Fortunately, I am a member of the Pearson Boats blog on googlegroups.com and am connected with several owners of *Skylark's* sisterships. There were 104 Pearson 36-1s built from 1970 to 1975 and many of them were raced under IOR rules. Steve Thurston of Quantum Sails in Rhode Island was particularly helpful and shared all his racing measurements and polar diagrams.

This documentation included measurements and specifically righting moments. This documentation was submitted to the inspection agency and has satisfied them and no measuring of *Skylark* was necessary.

On November 3rd, 2013, I sailed *Skylark* eastwards across the IJsselmeer to the town of Lemmer. This was to make it more convenient for the inspector to come to the boat for the inspection. The sailing season in The Netherlands was winding down and it was easy to find a berth along a dock in the center of town.

The dockmaster came by as I was tying up *Skylark* and asked me if I need electricity.

Thanks to the Superwind, I didn't.

He asked me if I need a shower and I didn't.

He said I could stay for free.

I told him I was awaiting a PCA inspection in the morning and he said "No problem".

The following afternoon, the inspector

arrived and started by just looking over *Skylark* from the dock. Then he walked around the deck. I offered him lunch, but he settled for a coffee. I didn't speak to him unless he asked me a question and after half an hour, he started pointing out *Skylark's* "defects".

The first item on his slowly growing list was that I would have to install a second lifeline under the top lifeline. This would simply entail drilling holes in all the stanchions, adding small nylon bushings to prevent wear on the lifeline or the stanchion and end the new lifeline with small turnbuckles.

Skylark's bow and stern railings already had loops welded to them, anticipating a second lifeline. The ORC requires that the lifelines be quickly disconnectable to facilitate hauling a person out of the water onto the deck.

I added pelican hooks to the aft end of all four lifelines.

The second point he mentioned was that although my two cockpit seat lids were lockable, they would benefit by the addition of a foam gasket to reduce the possibility of water ingress in a knockdown or a rollover. The hatch over the stern rope locker had a Nicro Solar Vent that has seen better days and that would have to be sealable so it wouldn't turn into a six inch hole in the deck. I would also have to fit a locking system to that hatch.

I added a beautiful Buck-Algonquin bronze deckplate and a flush locking mechanism.

Then he asked me where was the circuit for the bilge pump. I explained that during the electrical renovations, we had decided to wire the bilge pump and its float switch directly to a buss that was always hot. The inspector said that the bilge pump had to be able to be turned off in the event of oil spilling into the bilge and being pumped over.

My extremely well-maintained diesel engine doesn't leak any oil or fuel and I am always very careful, when changing fluids. Nonetheless, I installed a keyed switch and the bilge pump will stay on its own circuit.

The ventilation openings under the deck's dorade boxes that were on the main cabin's overhead and in the head would also have to be closable. I will installed small stainless steel rosettes on the overhead that I will be able to close with screwed-in plates when the weather gets rough.

Conclusion

I compiled this informaion and wrote this book in hope that it will encourage others to follow my and Cap'n Fatty's footsteps. There are pros and cons, differing opinions and different circumstances for anyone interested in owning a boat, building a boat, renovating a boat.

I don't claim to have all the answers, have bought the very best equipment or know everything to know about boat restoration. I have renovated two Pearsons in 40 years of sailing and learned from my mistakes. I was also lucky in that I did both of these renovation projects in a BOATYARD.

There is so much information on the internet about different projects, almost all the manuals for onboard equipment are now available as .pdf files to read for installations and operation.

Don Vanderveer, the boatyard owner, is a walking encyclopedia of marine engineering know-how. Charles Schwendler is a certified aircraft mechanic and knows everything about marine diesels. Andy Heermans, a recording engineer, somewhere along the line, learned professional wiring methods and was instrumental in installing all the systems from the boat's wiring to the LPG system.

We followed ABYC and Coast Guard specifications and no matter how daunting the task at hand, we were never tempted to cut any corners.

Trying to calculate lengths of cable runs, what gauge to use, how to attach cable and hose supports ever 12 inches without drilling holes into the underside of the deck were all problems that needed solutions.

I am a voracious reader and for the past 40 years have been constantly reading and researching best methods and products. What to do and how to do it and what not to do. What procedures and techniques were best was discussed in details with the mentors.

I have to apologize for the brevity of the text regarding the actual sail from Long Island, NY to Enkhuizen in The Netherlands. Not only is there a dearth of text, there aren't many photos.

The SPOT device that got us in trouble with the Canadian Coast Guard, plotted our daily fixes that The Mate's twin brother in Cincinatti plotted on a Google map and emailed the map daily to our families and friends who were on our mailing list.

As captain, I had many responsibilities, taking snapshots and keeping a detailed log had, unfortunately, lower priorities. We did make a lot of short videos with our small digital cameras. Most of the videos were of small whales and dolphins that would accompany us from time to time. On the rare occasion that we saw a ship or a fishing boat, we would get excited and shoot some footage.

Once we left Cape Race in Newfoundland, the air and sea temperature seemed to be the same. About 8°C or 47°F, it was just like Jerry Hodgens had predicted, COLD.

We had warm enough clothing, warm enough sleeping bags, but with the leaking toerail, things got wet and it was an effort to keep dry.

Off-watch was usually spent in our sleeping

bags, reading or sleeping. The night shifts were dreaded, not that it was dark, just cold and lonely.

Remember that due to the malfunctioning autopilot, we had to hand steer for the next 13 days across the ocean.

We were very lucky with the weather, but I like to think that that was because our departure was well-timed. Even though we lost half of our fresh water supply, good planning meant that we had twice as much as we needed.

We had plenty of food, but our shortage and lack of variety in canned meats, means I won't eat canned ham the rest of my life.

Our Eno Gasgone gimballed oven functioned perfectly. It was never so rough we couldn't use it. The fiddles used to hold pots and pans in place worked very well and were necessary. We had a Forespar gimballed storm burner and only used it to dry our wet gloves. When, on rare occasions, we ran the Yanmar, we would hang wet clothing in the engine compartment to dry.

The actual ocean crossing seemed endless, but it was 13 days of vigilence on the boat's systems and the crew's condition. We clipped our harnesses to the cockpit's padeyes when we were on night watch and our bunks either had leeboards or leecloths, so our sleep was sound.

Aside from the The Mate almost being keelhauled for his misuse of his own SPOT device, the crew got along very well.

The Mate, whose primary function in my mind was to splice and whip bitter ends of all the new line we had on board, had instead designated himself, the "communications officer" and after his fiasco with the SPOT device, I decided he was spending too much time and energy sending personal emails and downloading weather reports too often. Storm warnings are fine when a storm is coming, but one doesn't need to update the weather picture hourly.

Most of the crossing from Newfoundland was with westerly winds as predicted by the North Atlantic Pilot Chart for June and July. Only when we neared the west coast of Ireland did the wind change from west to southeast. I think that the wind god just wanted us to know who was boss for the last three days before our landing in Baltimore.

Skylark has quite a few years of cruising Europe and Scandinavia ahead of her. There are plenty of places on my "to visit" list. My long dreamed of circumnavigation has been put on the back burner, I am not keen on meeting pirates in the world's various hotspots. When my two sons are finished with high school, I could imagine doing an Atlantic circuit over a couple of years. We rushed past Canada, Ireland and the south coast of England and I would prefer spending time in the nicer spots around the Atlantic coastline.

The Suppliers that offered discounts or exceptional service:

www.defendermarine.com - Offers trade discounts or discounts on large purchases within one year.

www.westmarine.com - Has a division called Port Supply. Contact them for information about volume or trade discounts. Also, being a member of Boat/US ($35 a year) gets a 10% discount from West Marine.

http://www.pacergroup.net/ - offered great discounts on high quality electrical connectors and cable. They have a wide selection of material and tools. For wire that is equal to or superior to Ancor brand and at about 1/3 the price. They have everything for AYBC electrical standards. Great folks, they really worked with me on the complete rewiring of Skylark.

http://bluesea.com/ - Blue Sea - makes superior circuit panels, thru deck or bulkhead clams for wires, battery selectors and so on. Great quality, not cheap. Made in USA.

http://www.indelmarineusa.com/ -Isotemp water heater - sell made water heater that fit thru the lazarette. I was able to change the heating coil to 220 volts for about $50. Good worldwide service.

www.promariner.com/ - ProMariner sells an

excellent line of waterproof marine battery chargers. They replaced my water-damaged charger completely even after the warranty was expired.

www.hallspars.com - Hall Spars - Nan Hall was most helpful in finding a sheave for my boom exit box that had severe UV damage. They also found me a outhaul car that was exactly like my original, that had broken under stress...

www.rigrite.com - RigRite has many NOS marine fittings. I bought a traveller car, when my original got lost. I bought chain plate covers and a small tang that I used for making a lock for my companionway hatch. They even had parts for *Skylark's* original roller furler, but I changed to a Schaefer. RigRite is NOT cheap, but if they don't have it, you don't need it.

http://www.lewmar.com - Lewmar makes great hatches, I bought their V2 windlass. Their service wasn't very knowledgeable, but they have quality products

http://www.mackboring.com - Mack Boring for everything Yanmar.

http://www.tidesmarine.com - Tides Marine sells dripless flexible stuffing boxes Sure Seal and Strong Seal, plus motor mounts and flexible couplings.

http://store.marinepartdepot.com - stainless steel marine fittings at super low prices. Quality is acceptable. Always running sales. I bought massive skene chocks, large cleates, padeyes and so on.

http://www.superwind.com/ - SuperWind 350 is the most powerful and highest quality wind generator made.

Very quiet, actually it is too quiet. I often have to look to see if it is running or do I have the brakes on and puts out up to 27 amps per hour. Able to withstand 100 mph winds. In high wind conditions, the blades feather. This unit has saved my butt on several occasions. It is the most expensive of the genre, but I am seeing it on quality boats, research vessels and I have even seen it on data gathering buoys.

http://www.balmar.net/ - Balmar offers high output marine grade alternators and charging systems

http://www.lanocote.com/ - Lanocote lanolin-based grease for corrosion prevention. Keeps the stainless steel jaw of my spinnaker pole moving freely after we had to cut the jaw end off to get it to work freely to begin with. LanoCote® is the choice of marine professionals for long term corrosion control. This product is extremely effective in preventing and stopping corrosion on all types of metals under all environmental conditions.

List of upgrades

- Blue Sea modular circuit board with DC digital amp meter and 16 circuits

- Promariner multivoltage Protech1240iPlus 40 amp 3 bank charger

- Pacer Marine wire, cable and connectors - all gauges were one size larger than specified. All installed to ABYC code.

- Isotherm Basic 20 water heater - holds 6 gallons. Works from shore power, easily changeable heating element allows for different voltages. Also stores hot water heated by the engine.

- Dometic CF-110 refrigerator freezer - multivoltage 12-240V, stores 110 liters as a freezer or a refrigerator. Portable, yet easily mounted for stability.

- Raymarine navigation system - C120 MFD, windspeed, wind direction, depth sounder, SPX-5 wheelpilot, fluxgate compass, AIS class B transponder, Ray049 VHF radio, 24" radom

- SuperWind 350 - very high output, extremely quiet, durable marinized construction, high wind stability. Electric brake and voltage regulator. They give great service!

- Installed Eno Gasgogne gimballed stove and

oven. Three burners w/ pot fiddles. Galley strap and crash bar installed. Bakes well, easy to clean.

- Installed 1/4" aluminum plate behind the companionway boards to reinforce companionway against boarding waves.

- Install oversized teak toerails using bolts, nuts and washers to replace the original screws.

- Installed Schaefer 2100 roller furler

- New Quantum mainsail - not for racing, rather bulletproof

- Lewmar V2 windlass, with chainstopper and Bowline bow roller.

- Manson Supreme 45lb anchor with 100ft 3/8 chain spliced to 200ft 12-plait 5/8" line.

- replaced standing rigging and used bronze and stainless turnbuckles and Sta-Lok fittings on the deck end.

- Added second lifeline under original.

- Added second antenna for second VHF and AIS transponder.

- Replaced old Lewmar sheet winches with Anderson ST40s.

- Replaced coaming caps with 1" teak fixed with nuts and bolts.

- 1/4" and 1/2" HDPE used as backing plates for all deck fittings.

- Reinforced aftdeck to 1" thickness to support radar/ wind generator mast and oversize stainless steel tangs for Jordan Series drogue attachment points.

- Painted old TreadMaster with TreadMasters deck restorer and had unsatisfactory results. Repainted with Interdeck and had better results.

- Painted any exposed fiberglass on the deck, cabin top and cockpit cockpit with POR-15 WhiteCote. Also painted a 1/2" strip on the deck level of the inboard side of the new toe rail to seal the Sikaflex adhesive/sealer from any contact with cleaning chemicals and freezing water.

- Replaced brakes and needle bearings on Edson pedestal axle - first time in 37 years.

- Replaced seal on StrongSeal flexible shaft seal.

- Replaced packing in rudder stuffing box - first time in 37 years. To avoid damaging the threaded cap on the top of the rudder stuffing box, I placed a large stainless hose clamp around the flat hexagon of the cap to protect the bronze cap from being scratched by a large set of locking pliers. Then I placed a small hydraulic jack between the rudder stop and the pliers and forced the cap to turn off - first time in 37 years.

- Disassembled, cleaned and regreased all bronze Wilcox-Crittenden seacocks - first time in 37 years

- Installed holding tank, new Jabsco toilet, new sanitary hoses with "Y" valve.

- Pulled and rebedded all chainplates.

- Removed old laminated hull liner and replaced with Miranti lathing painted ivory to match the overhead and secured with bronze #8 screws and finish washers.

- Replaced reading lights with LED bulbs

- Replaced deck light, anchor light and running lights with LED. Only the steaming light and two overhead lights are still tungsten.

- Replaced original Yanmar 35 amp alternator with a Balmar 70 amp alternator eventually upgrading to a Balmar 100 amp alternator. Uses Balmar's ARS-5 regulator.

- Installed Flex-o-Fold two blade propeller, the manufacturer originally sent me a 16" model that was too big for the allowed space. They changed the blades to 15" models.

- Added an Isoflex flexible coupling that required the propeller shaft to be shortened by the length of the coupling's thickness and a new keyway to be cut.

MASTER CARPENTER'S CERTIFICATE
(BUILDER'S CERTIFICATE)

DEPARTMENT OF TRANSPORTATION
U. S. COAST GUARD
CG-1261 (Rev. 6-67)

Form Approved Bureau of Budget No. 04-R3038

PLACE: Portsmouth, R.I.
DATE: June 28, 1974
NAME OF MASTER OR PRINCIPAL CARPENTER: William H. Shaw
ADDRESS: West Shore Road, Portsmouth, Rhode Island 02871
RIG: Sloop Rig - Gas Screw Yacht
NAME OF THE VESSEL:
HULL NO.: #58 (Pearson-36) (PEA510580473)
VESSEL WAS BUILT: by Pearson Yachts Division of Grumman Allied Industries, Inc.
YEAR OF COMPLETION: 1973
PLACE WHERE BUILT: Portsmouth, Rhode Island
MATERIAL OF BUILD: Fiberglass

NAME OF PERSON OR PERSONS FOR WHOM BUILT AND INDIVIDUAL INTEREST OWNED

McMichael International, Ltd.
447 East Boston Post Road
Mamaroneck, New York 10543

NUMBER OF DECKS	NUMBER OF MASTS	CONTOUR OF STEM	SHAPE OF STERN
One	One	Curved	Elliptical

LENGTH OF VESSEL: 36' 6-3/4" FEET
BREADTH OF VESSEL: 11' 1-1/4" FEET
DEPTH OF VESSEL: 7' 3-3/4" FEET
GROSS TONNAGE: 14.8
NET TONNAGE: 13.4

THE FOLLOWING ADDITIONAL PARTICULARS SHALL BE GIVEN FOR THE ENGINE OF MACHINERY-PROPELLED VESSELS

TYPE OF ENGINE: Gas - Internal Combustion
PLACE WHERE BUILT: Oshkosh, Wisconsin
YEAR BUILT: 1973
BUILT BY: Universal Motors Division Medalist Industries, Inc.
POWER: Gasoline   Serial #180136

NOTE.—An *oil* engine is an internal-combustion engine in which the fuel is injected into the air that is under compression in the cylinder; the combination is ignited by the heat generated from the compression (Diesel type), or from additional outside heat when that in the cylinder is not sufficient (Semi-Diesel type). A *gas* engine is also an internal combustion engine, but in it the fuel and air are admitted into the cylinder simultaneously and the combination is ignited by a spark.

I certify that the information given above is true and correct to the best of my knowledge and belief.

A certified copy of Skylark's Master Carpenter's Certificate. The original was filed with the US Coast Guard's Documentation Center. Athought the Dutch VAT was paid and she has been CE marked, Skylark is still a US documented vessel flying the Stars and Stripes.

Skylark on her first European mooring.
Baltimore, Ireland
June 26, 2009

www.ingramcontent.com/pod-product-compliance
Lightning Source LLC
Chambersburg PA
CBHW050557300426
44112CB00013B/1963